IN FOCUS

Developing a Working Relationship with Your Performance Dog

Fun, Obedience, and Consistency Lead to Unbelievable Success

By Deborah Jones, Ph.D. & Judy Keller

IN FOCUS: *Developing a Working Relationship with Your Performance Dog*

For information contact:
Clean Run Productions, LLC
35 N. Chicopee St. Unit 4
Chicopee, MA 01020
Phone: 413-532-1389 or 800-311-6503
Fax: 413-532-1590
Website: www.cleanrun.com

Edited by Nini Bloch, Monica Percival, Marcille Ripperton, and Lisa Baird

Cover photo by Joe Canova

Back cover photo by Pup Art/Kathleen Schaffer

Book Design and Typesetting by Anne Cusolito

Cover Design by Anne Cusolito

First edition

First printing October 2004

ISBN 1-892694-11-5

Dedication

This book would not be possible without all the dogs that have taught us so much, especially Katie, Sully, Copper, Luna, Morgan, Sabre, and Smudge. In particular, this book is dedicated to Quest, who made a short but incredible journey through our hearts.

Deb and Judy

Table of Contents

Preface

Over the past 10 years, the sport of dog agility has become increasingly popular in the United States. Many dog training groups and clubs are offering agility classes and hosting agility trials. And in many parts of the country those classes and trials fill almost immediately. One of the reasons cited for this phenomenon is that agility is fun for both the dog and the owner. While this is often true, unfortunately it isn't always the case. Many dogs can meet the physical demands required for agility (given proper training and conditioning), but they might have more difficulty with the mental aspects of the game. Agility requires concentration, confidence, and a willingness to take direction from and work with a handler. For some dog and handler pairs this working partnership may develop naturally over the course of training, but for many it does not. The result is a dog that is physically capable of doing agility but that may be distracted, unmotivated, out of control, or inconsistent in the ring. This book is designed to address these problems and to help you and your dog become a better working team.

The FOCUS program is the foundation underlying your training relationship with your dog. FOCUS stands for Fun, Obedience, and Consistency lead to Unbelievable Success. This program addresses the fundamental requirements for a good working partnership between dog and trainer in an organized, systematic manner. It can help you build, rebuild, strengthen, or repair problems with concentration, confidence, and teamwork. The FOCUS program is a great way to start a new puppy, but it can also help with a dog of any age at any level of training. It's never too late to build FOCUS.

This book is *not* about training agility obstacles. We are assuming that you will be training obstacles in addition to working on your FOCUS program. This book is also *not* about agility handling. Our recommendation is that you find a good, experienced agility instructor who uses positive reinforcement techniques, such as clicker training. (We will explain and discuss clicker training in the "Foundation Focus" section of this book.) Ideally, you would start FOCUS work before agility training and would continue it throughout your dog's agility career. Sometimes it may be necessary to take a short break from agility training and trialing, lay a strong working foundation with your FOCUS program, and then integrate the two. We will talk about when this change might be necessary and how to do it.

While we are specifically discussing applications of the FOCUS program to agility, aspects of the program can be useful for any dog sport that requires teamwork and cooperation between dog and handler.

Acknowledgements

First, we would like to thank our mothers, Ruth Rice and Mildred Keller, for always encouraging and believing in us. We would like to thank Clean Run Productions, particularly Monica Percival, for giving us the opportunity to share our training ideas with others. In addition, we would like to thank our editor, Nini Bloch, for her extremely helpful insights and comments. Thanks also to our Toledo friends and critics, Kim Holmes and Joanne Silhanek, for their feedback.

Introductions

THE PEOPLE

Deb:

I have always enjoyed spending time with animals (often more than with people). In college I focused on studying learning processes and behavior and discovered that the laws of learning apply to all creatures that have a nervous system. In graduate school I got my first performance dog, a rescue Labrador Retriever. By trial and error Katie and I stumbled our way through obedience, agility, and pet therapy. In addition, Katie became a wonderful demo dog for my classes, learning a huge number of tricks. Through it all, I worked on developing training techniques that were positive, fun, and fair. I am now showing my Papillon Copper in obedience and agility. Copper recently earned his MACH and Utility Dog titles. My younger Papillon Luna(tic) is just starting her agility career.

Judy:

I have loved animals my whole life. Over the past 17 years I have owned 8 Shelties (not all at one time!). In 1995 I entered the world of performance with Morgan, an incredible dog. Morgan and I learned about agility training together. In 1997, 1998, and 1999, we competed on the U.S. AKC World Agility Team. In 1998 we were members of the gold-medal-winning mini-team. In January 2000 I got a puppy named Sabre as my next agility dog. Sabre introduced me to a whole new world of dog training. Unlike Morgan, who made everything easy, Sabre has made me work very, very hard. He has forced me to become a much better trainer and is the inspiration for this book.

THE DOGS

Throughout this book we will be highlighting our discussion of training concepts and techniques using examples of our own dogs and dogs we have worked with. We have used aspects of the FOCUS program while working with many dogs of different breeds, personalities, and training backgrounds.

Deb's Papillon, Copper, is a good example of a dog that needs a lot of work to maintain his enthusiasm and enjoyment in agility. While Copper is a quick learner and (usually) is very obedient, he easily becomes stressed and worried. Once stressed or worried, Copper is no longer having fun and does not work well. He needs training methods that build his confidence and strengthen his skills by allowing him to be successful at each step. Too much pressure or too many errors cause him to slow down, shut down, and stop working.

Sabre is Judy's young Sheltie and the inspiration for putting the FOCUS program on paper. We will be referring to **Sabre's Story** throughout this book. A fast and motivated dog, Sabre was having too much fun in the ring. He ignored his partnership with Judy in favor of the adrenaline rush of running. After working diligently through the FOCUS program, Sabre has lost none of his speed and drive*, and Judy has gained his complete attention and cooperation while working. Now Judy says, "Sabre has gone from *running around* the ring to *working* in the ring." He has developed into an intense and focused working partner for Judy.

*Note: We are using the term **drive** in this book in the informal, not the scientific, sense. We are using it as shortcut to describe a dog that is highly and intrinsically motivated to train and perform. The term, used in this context, has nothing to do with scientific or non-scientific drive theories.*

Copper and Sabre are at opposite ends of the 'agility personality' scales. Copper is always in danger of *not having any or enough fun*, and Sabre is often on the verge of *having too much fun*. To train and compete successfully, these dogs need trainers that understand their unique challenges and that use techniques to maximize their strengths and address their areas of weakness. Fortunately, the FOCUS program is flexible enough to allow us to individualize training plans that are effective for each type of dog.

What is FOCUS?

Sabre's Story: Why he needed the FOCUS program

©PUP ART BY KATHLEEN SCHAFFER

Judy was sick and tired of not qualifying at agility trials. Sabre seemed to be stuck and unable to earn an Excellent Standard leg. His mental, not his physical state, was the problem. Although he is an athletic, driven, fast dog, he seemed unable to concentrate and follow direction. Judy had plenty of advice on what to do, including removing him from competition for several months to give him the opportunity to mature. Unfortunately, it often doesn't work this way. Time alone does not make up for a lack of foundation training.

While natural speed and drive are wonderful attributes in an agility dog, they are not enough on their own. Sabre did not understand the concept of teamwork. If agility were simply a foot race, he would have won hands down. Negotiating the obstacles according to Judy's direction was not part of Sabre's understanding of the game. We needed to teach him that working with Judy was more rewarding than the adrenaline rush of running around the ring.

WHAT IS FOCUS?

There are three main working parts to the FOCUS program: Fun, Obedience, and Consistency. These three parts lead to the finished product: Unbelievable Success! While the program requires sustained effort, the results are worth it. FOCUS is the interaction between the dog and trainer, the line of communication that opens and develops between them. It requires concentration and hard work from both. Developing FOCUS involves taking the time to establish a new way of relating to your dog both in training and in daily life. In the FOCUS program, you will increase your dog's general awareness of you and make yourself the most important element in the environment. You and your dog will engage in mutually enjoyable activities and build a stronger relationship. Your dog will learn that working for you leads to all the good things he wants. You will learn how to manage and control the environment in ways designed to gain greater willingness and compliance from your dog. The result is a dog that is eager, enthusiastic, and readily responsive.

Trainers often talk about teaching the dog to pay attention. By attention, they typically mean teaching the dog to respond to a cue by looking at the trainer. This cue might be used when the dog is distracted or unresponsive. While FOCUS involves an increase in attention from the dog, it is different from simply asking the dog to *Watch* for a short period. FOCUS is ongoing while attention is discrete. Attention has a beginning (triggered by the cue), a period of expected compliance (the behavior), and an end (the release). FOCUS, on the other hand, is in play during all interactions between dog and handler. There is no formal cue for FOCUS, but there are many informal signals that indicate to the dog that he should be paying closer attention to the trainer. Gaining attention is the responsibility of the trainer, not the dog. The trainer initiates the cue, the dog responds, and the trainer releases. With FOCUS, it is the dog's responsibility to maintain awareness of the trainer. The trainer doesn't ask for FOCUS; the dog offers it.

The dog always has a primary focus. He can be focusing mainly on the trainer, on the environment, or on himself.* While our goal is to increase trainer focus, there are times when it is necessary for the dog to switch his attention to the environment or to himself.

*Note: Pati and Stuart Mah have discussed a basic distinction between handler and obstacle focus. Our concept of focus takes this idea further to consider the broader aspects of the environment as well as an internal self-focus.

Environmental focus involves paying more attention to things in the outside world, such as the agility obstacles themselves. For example, a dog that, on a cue from his handler, moves forward to take a line of jumps is focusing appropriately on the environment at that time. He must switch from handler to environmental focus quickly to perform correctly.

On the other hand, a dog that spies an off-course tunnel across the agility field and takes off on his own to perform it is not in the desired focus at that moment.

Despite entreaties from his handler, a dog with too much obstacle focus has decided the off-course seesaw is HIS choice.

Trying to train—or run—a dog whose mind is elsewhere is a waste of time.

He has chosen environmental focus over handler focus. Environmental focus can also be a problem when the dog is paying attention to all the activity and distractions around him rather than to the handler. A dog that runs out of the agility ring to chase birds is a good example. Attempting to train or show a dog that is in strong environmental focus is usually a waste of time. The dog cannot concentrate on the handler and on himself since he is too busy being "out in the world" mentally.

To be successful in agility, there are times when the dog must switch his focus to himself. This internal focus is necessary when the dog needs to concentrate on what he is physically doing at the moment. For example, weave pole performance requires the dog to be highly aware of his body movements because weaving is not natural for dogs. A two-on/two-off contact performance is another situation where the dog needs to switch to an internal focus to get his body in the correct position.

Internal focus can be a problem when it is the result of stress and anxiety. If the dog is overwhelmed by unpleasant internal sensations, he will not be able to pay attention to the handler or to the required task. His reactions to his internal state will block learning and lead to poor performance of known behaviors.

A mature, confident, well-trained agility dog has learned to quickly and appropriately switch focus when necessary. For example, when performing the weaves the dog uses all three types of focus. First, the dog needs handler focus to be aware of the cue to weave. The dog must then switch to environmental focus to find and move toward the correct obstacle. Then, the dog must switch to self-focus to perform weaving behavior correctly.

Sabre was a good example of a dog that had an extremely strong environmental focus. On the agility field Sabre lost all handler focus and went into something

A dog with too much handler focus while weaving will have a hard time concentrating on the muscle patterns necessary to complete the poles.

Julie Daniels once labeled *run mode*. That involved going full speed around the course but only taking obstacles he considered easy and fun. By applying the FOCUS program, we increased Sabre's handler- and self-focus, which led to vastly improved agility performances. We knew we were successful when he could be redirected even when heading full speed toward a tunnel (his favorite obstacle).

Copper, on the other hand, is sometimes too handler- and self-focused, making him slower and more careful. Teaching him to become more focused on the environment and to move ahead boldly was the challenge. We knew we were successful when he confidently and quickly took an off-course tunnel, even when Deb was desperately trying to redirect him. (Even though Copper failed to qualify on that run, it was a success in terms of our long-term goals of more speed and confidence for Copper.)

WHO CAN BENEFIT?

Everyone! FOCUS is helpful to anyone who wants to develop a better working partnership with his or her dog. It is especially useful to those who engage in performance sports such as agility and obedience, and for those who are involved in pet therapy visits and programs. If your dog is not as attentive, enthusiastic, and responsive as you would like, FOCUS can help. In this book we shall be using agility as the primary focus and drawing most of our examples from that performance sport. You can apply the same principles to improve the working relationship with your canine partner, whatever your choice of performance sport or activity.

WHY DO YOU NEED FOCUS?

You need FOCUS to build a strong and successful working relationship with your dog. FOCUS is an important foundation regardless of the actual activities you would like to teach. Once you have FOCUS, it will be much easier to train any and all behaviors. Your dog will be eager and willing to work with you.

While it is possible to train a dog without FOCUS, it is more difficult than it needs to be. Constantly working to keep the dog's attention and competing with all sorts of distractions in the environment is tiring, aggravating, and a waste of valuable training time. A dog with FOCUS is ready to learn. The FOCUS program lays the groundwork by establishing clear guidelines for acceptable behavior from the dog, opening a communication channel between dog and trainer, and making sure it is in the dog's best interest to cooperate.

THE FOCUS PHILOSOPHY

We have designed the FOCUS program as a way to enhance the relationship and communication between dog and trainer. The FOCUS program is based on respect for dogs and a dedication to positive and gentle training techniques. We believe that dogs are intelligent and sensitive creatures, and we feel that force and intimidation in training are counterproductive to a true working partnership. FOCUS techniques give dogs an opportunity to learn in a stress-free and relaxed manner. They also allow the trainer to gain control of the dog's behavior with the dog's complete cooperation during the training process.

How to Read Your Dog

Understanding your dog's personality and accurately interpreting the underlying causes of his behavior will help you design an effective agility-training program. Observing and reading your dog's behavior is a skill that takes time to develop. While it is fairly easy to see *what* the dog is doing, knowing *why* the dog is behaving in a certain way is much more difficult. Explanations for the causes of a dog's behavior are often inaccurate. We simply cannot know with 100% certainty why the dog is behaving in any particular way. Behaviorists call the brain a *black box* that we cannot see into. Since we cannot get into our dogs' heads to ask them, our explanations for the causes of their behaviors are simply guesses at best, and our guesses may be wrong.

Although you know your dog better than anyone, it can be hard to be clear and objective in your assessment of his behavior and personality. We are all biased because we are so close to our dogs. Sometimes people have pre-existing notions that color all their interpretations of a dog's behavior. For example, "He's a sighthound; of course he's going to be distracted," or "She's just being stubborn; she's a dominant dog." It may be beneficial to ask several other people to help categorize your dog based on the listings below. You might be surprised at their interpretations of your dog's behavior.

The following lists of behaviors and tendencies are based on our observations in training classes and at trials and are designed to help you determine what type of agility dog you have. That determination will help guide you in applying the FOCUS program to best fit the needs of your own dog. The general distinctions are *not having any or enough fun* or *having too much fun*. These are simple subjective categories.

While some of the descriptions concern temperament (innate personality), others simply reflect lack of training or environmental issues. For example, your dog may not hold a start-line stay because of a lack of training. Or he may not hold a start-line stay because he is so excited about getting moving. Or he may not hold a start-line stay because the dog behind him is making him nervous. In all these cases the answer is the same: more training. But the causes of the problem and the solutions required are different.

Also, remember that you know your dog in many different situations and settings. An overall evaluation of behavior and temperament would allow you to look at the "whole dog" and get a more accurate view.

The descriptions that follow are based on agility, but you may see similar behaviors in other activities, such as obedience.

DOGS THAT AREN'T HAVING ANY OR ENOUGH FUN

Signs that your dog isn't having enough fun:
Once you've ruled out physical problems…
Your dog performs agility slowly, sometimes not making standard course time.
Your dog seems distracted and disinterested while doing agility.
Your dog sniffs, scratches, and/or yawns before and during agility.
Your dog regularly avoids obstacles during an agility run.
Your dog seems to "zone out" and wanders off on his own during training and/or trials.

Dos and don'ts for dogs that aren't having enough fun:

DON'T "cheerlead" your dog.
Constant encouragement to increase speed and take each obstacle will backfire in the long run. At first your dog's speed will increase slightly, but then he will slow down again. Then cheerleading will be necessary to get him to run at all.

DO use well-placed praise and verbal rewards.
Praise and rewards come AFTER the desired behavior; they are not meant to cause it. Quiet, sincere verbal praise marks a job well done.

DON'T correct or scold your dog for errors.
Consider all mistakes to be your fault, not the dog's fault. The error was either in your training, your handling, or an overwhelming environment. Scolding a dog that already has little confidence and motivation will only make matters worse. Sometimes even mild expressions of disappointment are enough to slow down this type of dog even more.

DO set your dog up for success.
If your dog can't be successful, he will give up and stop trying. Your job is to plan training sessions carefully so that he is highly likely to do well. Increasing your dog's chances for success may include going back to square one and retraining an exercise or obstacle. While retraining may be time-consuming, it will increase your dog's confidence and his enjoyment of the game.

"Star-gazing" at the top of the A-frame is a typical expression of lack of confidence, distraction, or stress—all signs of a dog that is not having enough fun.

DON'T push your dog to his limits.

Dogs that lack motivation and confidence need to be carefully nurtured. Your training sessions should always be short and exciting. Long classes and sequences may be too much both physically and mentally. Even just hanging out ringside may be overwhelming and mentally tiring for some dogs.

DO stop before your dog wants to.

Mini-sessions are best for dogs that need more motivation. One-to-three obstacle sequences, sandwiched between play and food jackpots, will help your dog form a positive mental association with agility performance.

DON'T make training/showing serious business.

Sensitive dogs are quick to pick up on the moods of their trainers. If you are tense, stressed, or too serious in training, your dog will be even more inhibited.

DO make training and showing seem like play.

Your dog shouldn't be able to tell where play ends and work begins. This is much harder for the trainer but absolutely necessary for certain dogs.

If your dog isn't having enough fun, you need to concentrate on the exercises and activities suggested in the "Fun" section of this book first. Once your dog is clearly enjoying time spent training, then you can work more on the necessary obedience exercises.

DOGS THAT ARE HAVING TOO MUCH FUN

Signs that your dog is having too much fun:

Your dog eagerly and enthusiastically zooms around the ring, not listening to direction.

Your dog chooses his own course.

Your dog visits the judge, stewards, and so on when he should be running the course. Rather than seeing agility as an athletic event, your dog views it as a social event.

You cannot get your dog to pay attention to you when he is close to the ring, when another dog is running, or immediately before an agility run.

Your dog cannot hold a start-line or table stay.

Note: Sometimes it is difficult to tell the difference between a dog that is having too much fun and a dog that is stressed and practicing avoidance behaviors (such as running around rather than focusing on agility obstacles). It takes someone with an open mind and good observational skills to tell the difference. Stressed dogs are not having too much fun, just the opposite. Again, it is a good idea to ask someone you respect to observe your dog and give you an objective interpretation.

Dos and don'ts for dogs that are having too much fun:

DON'T ignore the problem.
A lack of control will not disappear on its own or go away with time. Be honest and admit that your dog needs some foundation work. You will be much more successful if you address the problem sooner rather than later.

©DAVID RAMEY PHOTOGRAPHY

This dog has invented his own, consistent, blazingly fast, and self-reinforcing style of doing the weave poles. Is he having too much fun? You be the judge.

DO start an obedience-training program based on positive reinforcement.
Obedience doesn't have to be overwhelmingly strict to be effective. It may be a challenge to make obedience training fun, but it can be done.

DON'T allow your dog to continue practicing inappropriate and incorrect behaviors.
Remember, practice makes perfect. Every time you go into an agility ring and your dog doesn't follow your directions, the habit of *not listening while doing agility* becomes stronger and stronger.

DO remove your dog from competition while working on basic training problems.
In the short run you will save all that money you are spending on non-qualifying runs. In the long run you will have a much better chance of reaching the higher levels of agility and being consistently successful. A short hiatus to address problems can be critical. Continuing to show a dog when you cannot control undesirable behaviors will negate your training efforts outside the ring.

DON'T settle for physical control of your dog.
Most dogs are controllable when wearing a leash and collar, but agility is a hands-off sport. If your dog bolts when you remove the leash, you haven't done your training homework and you shouldn't be in the show ring yet.

DO develop psychological control of your dog.
Psychological control involves convincing the dog that he wants to be with you and work with you, even when he has other options. To gain this control you need a strong and consistent reinforcement history in which your dog knows that you can provide all the good things he wants.

DON'T blame your dog.
Dogs will do whatever is the most reinforcing in the environment. It's not his fault that he finds agility on his own terms more fun than agility on your terms. Resist the urge to blame your dog's behavior on his personality or temperament. Your dog's behavior is a product of your training (or lack thereof).

DO make yourself and your activities more interesting to your dog.
Again, dogs will do whatever is the most reinforcing in the environment. Are you making agility fun, or are you making it boring? Does your dog enjoy playing with you outside of agility? Nurture a relationship based on mutual enjoyment away from agility, and then incorporate it into your training program.

If your dog is having too much fun, you need to concentrate on the exercises and activities suggested in the "Obedience" section of this book first. Once your dog is under better control, you can incorporate more of the fun exercises into your training program.

Foundation FOCUS

You will need to do some foundation work so that you can get the most benefit possible from the FOCUS program. Consider this foundation work as the best way to prepare yourself and your dog for the activities, exercises, and suggestions that will follow. Investing the time and energy in a good foundation will definitely be worth the effort.

LEARNING HOW TO LEARN

Before you start agility training, it is helpful to lay the groundwork that will prepare your dog to learn quickly and easily. *Learning how to learn* is a general concept that you can help your dog understand in the early stages of training. The basis of learning how to learn is teaching your dog that his actions control the things that happen to him. Dogs are opportunists and will take advantage of whatever has the best outcome. Why does a dog jump up on the kitchen counter and steal food? Because it has a positive outcome for him: he gets steak. We can use a dog's natural opportunism to our advantage by teaching our dogs that specific behaviors will lead to positive outcomes while other behaviors lead to negative outcomes. Understanding that there is a predictable relationship between a dog's actions and their consequences will create a *thinking* dog, one that attempts to manipulate his environment through his behavior. The dog is learning to be what B.F. Skinner called *operant*. He is operating on the environment to obtain the desired outcome. We, as trainers, are essential because we can provide the outcomes. In a sense, we are the middlemen in this process. Our role is not to cause the dog to behave in a certain way. Instead, it is to observe the dog's behavior and be ready to provide the appropriate outcome or consequence.

When Luna was a puppy, for example, Deb wanted her to learn to wait in her crate after the door was opened until she was given a verbal release. To teach the wait, all Deb had to do was control the outcome based on Luna's behavior. She would only begin to open the crate door when Luna was still. If Luna moved, Deb closed the door and waited. When Luna was still Deb continued opening the door. Luna learned quickly that she could cause Deb to open the crate door if she held still. Luna was learning what it meant to be operant and to control the things that happened to her.

OPERANT CONDITIONING

Operant conditioning (OC) is the basis for much of the learning that occurs in dog training. OC is all about consequences. Learning occurs because certain behaviors lead to certain consequences. Scientists have studied this type of learning as far back as the late 1800s, when Edward Thorndike discovered what he called *The Law of Effect*. Thorndike's experiments involved placing a cat inside a "puzzle box." Inside the box was a lever that would open the box and allow the cat to escape (and the cats were highly motivated to escape). The researchers placed a cat in the box and recorded the time it took the cat to discover that pressing the lever led to being released. At first the cat tried other behaviors, such as scratching, howling, and jumping around, none of which worked. By chance he hit the lever and escaped. Again the scientists placed the cat in the box and recorded the time to escape. They repeated the trial until the cat was hitting the lever as soon as he was put into the box. The cat had discovered that none of the other behaviors (scratching, howling, and jumping around) were useful in producing the desired effect, so those behaviors disappeared. Instead he started repeating the behavior that worked, hitting the lever, as soon as possible. According to Thorndike, the effect of the behavior determined whether the cat would repeat it. Ineffective behaviors, or those that produce unpleasant consequences, disappear. On the other hand, effective behaviors, those that produce desired consequences, increase. These basic concepts govern OC.

MARK THE MOMENT

To use the FOCUS program effectively, it is vital to consistently use a behavioral marker in your training. A behavioral marker is a signal (such as a click, word, or other sound) that indicates the specific action you are rewarding. This will help to establish a clear line of communication with your dog. Using a behavioral marker will speed up your training progress tremendously.

Adding a behavioral marker to the process makes it clear to the dog that a specific behavior is being reinforced. When possible, we prefer to use a clicker as that behavioral marker, but you also can use a short, clear word (such as *Yes*) as your verbal marker. Simply use your marker while the dog is exhibiting the desired behavior, and then offer the reinforcer. A well-timed mark clearly defines the moment for the dog and makes the desired behavior more likely to occur in the future. To be effective, however, you should always follow the marker with a reinforcer (food, toys, play, and so on).

Consequences, Consequences

In OC there are five possible outcomes to any behavior. These possibilities are *positive reinforcement, negative reinforcement, positive punishment, negative punishment,* or *no change* in the environment.

A behavior that produces a desired result (a positive reinforcer) will increase in frequency. When your dog sits and you give him a food treat you are using positive reinforcement. The pleasant consequence (the food) will increase the desired behavior (sitting).

A behavior that removes an unpleasant condition (a negative reinforcer) will also increase in frequency. When you are riding a horse and want him to stop, you pull back on the reins, which puts pressure on the metal bit in his mouth. When the horse stops (the desired behavior) you release the pressure (the unpleasant condition). The release is negative reinforcement.

A behavior that produces an unpleasant result (positive punishment) will decrease in frequency. When a parent spanks a child, the unpleasant consequence (spanking) is meant to decrease the undesired behavior. Positive punishment, however, has potentially serious side effects. The unpleasant emotional response due to punishment can actually inhibit rather than increase learning and can also lead to other undesired responses such as avoidance or aggression.

A behavior that removes a pleasant condition (negative punishment) will decrease in frequency. Taking away something your child wants (TV, video game, telephone use) to decrease an undesired behavior is an example of negative punishment. Taking away a child's freedom (being grounded) is the ultimate negative punishment.

A behavior that does not alter outcomes at all results in extinction (the behavior disappears). Unless the behavior is self-reinforcing (enjoyable in and of itself), it will decrease and disappear over time. Behaviors that have no effect are a waste of time and energy, but a self-reinforcing behavior, like barking, digging, or chewing, will probably continue and even increase.

There is abundant scientific evidence that demonstrates the predictable nature of these consequences. If a behavior is continuing or increasing, it is being maintained by reinforcement. If a behavior is decreasing or disappearing, it is being reduced by punishment or extinction. These are the basic laws of operant conditioning. When consequences are applied consistently and properly, behavior changes accordingly.

©CLEAN RUN

On the Mark

The purpose of a behavioral marker is to signal that a desired behavior has occurred. The marker is a communication tool. It gives your dog feedback on his behavior. It tells him "The thing you were doing at the moment you heard the mark is something I want you to repeat." It also tells him that a positive reinforcer is coming. In scientific terms the marker is referred to as either a conditioned or a secondary reinforcer because it gains its power by being connected with primary positive reinforcers such as food and play.

While anything the dog can sense (see, hear, or smell) can be used as a marker, some things work better than others. A marker needs to stand out in the environment, be easily perceived, and be easily controlled by the trainer. In the laboratory, rats and pigeons can be taught a range of behavioral markers including flashing colored lights, a wide variety of sounds, and even different scents (such as vanilla).

The most important characteristic of a good marker is that it predictably signals the presentation of a primary reinforcer. The marker must come first and be followed as closely in time as possible by the positive reinforcer. Especially when you first start training, you don't want anything else to happen between the mark and the reinforcement that might distract or confuse the dog. And you must always follow the mark with a reinforcer. Otherwise you weaken the connection you've established between the marker and the reinforcer, and the marker loses its power. The consistent use of a behavioral marker will definitely speed up your training by giving your dog information about the specific behavior he is being reinforced for.

CLICKER TRAINING

While clicker training is a new concept to some dog trainers, it has been around for a long time. In 1951 B.F. Skinner published an article in *Scientific American* titled "How to Train Animals" that was the first scientific description of clicker training techniques. The idea of using a clicker as a behavioral marker came about because of something scientists call the *magazine effect*. The magazine is the mechanism that holds and releases food pellets in a Skinner box (a Plexiglas cage used for experimental training). When the rat performed a desirable behavior, the experimenter released a food pellet. The magazine made a clicking sound as the food was released but before it reached the rat in his Skinner box. Scientists observed that the rats quickly learned to orient to the food tray when they heard the click of the magazine. The sound had become a behavioral marker. More important, scientists discovered that rats trained in ways that bypassed the sound of the magazine learned more slowly.

The clicker is a good behavioral marker because it is usually a novel sound, something most dogs have not heard before. Using more common sounds like a beep, a buzz, or a squeaker, is less effective because most dogs have learned to ignore those sounds in everyday life. A clicker is also a good behavioral marker because it is easily heard, even in noisy environments. Its sharp, distinct sound makes it a good choice. With a little practice, the trainer can click faster and more accurately than giving a verbal marker, like *Good*. This ability allows you to "catch" desired behavior as it occurs, which leads the dog to learn faster.

GUIDELINES FOR CLICKER TRAINING:

1. **Charge up the clicker by pairing a click and a treat.**
   Don't ask for any specific behaviors at first, just click–treat, click–treat, click–treat as fast as possible about 20 times. Simply be sure your dog isn't doing anything you don't like when you click.

2. **Don't click too close to your dog's ear!**
   It hurts, a lot. If your dog seems a little worried about the sound of the click, keep the clicker in your pocket or behind your back. If your dog still seems worried, try to find a soft clicker (they vary a lot in sharpness and volume). Some people recommend putting some masking tape over the metal part of the clicker to soften the sound. You can also use a ballpoint pen or a baby food jar lid for a softer click.

3. **Pair the clicker with toys and games in the same way you charged it up with treats.**
   Click and play for a short period, then repeat. It helps add variety to your reinforcers by pairing the clicker with all the things your dog loves.

4. **Always follow the click with a reinforcer. This needs to be a one-to-one relationship.**
   Clicking without offering a reinforcer lowers the value of the click as a signal that good things are coming and thus makes the meaning of the click inconsistent.

5. **Use the click as a behavioral marker.**
   The purpose of using the clicker is to mark the *exact* moment your dog performs a behavior you like. Believe it or not, the clicker is much more precise than the human voice. Moreover, people tend to chatter at the dog rather than use a single, short, distinctive word.

6. **Only click once for each desired behavior.**
Because the sound of the click is a precise behavioral marker, multiple clicks will be confusing to your dog.

7. **Practice your timing.**
Your training is only effective when you are exact in your behavioral mark. Most people click much too late. Practice your clicker timing by teaching silly tricks and playing shaping games such as 101 Things to Do with a Box (see "Clicker Fun" below)

8. **Split, don't lump.**
Build the behaviors you want to teach in a step-by-step manner. Break down each behavior into the smallest possible parts and teach each part separately. Expecting too much too soon will lead to failure.

HOW TO BE A "SPLITTER"

Splitters break behaviors down into tiny pieces and teach each piece individually. This practice helps your dog to be successful at each step in training. A dog that is successful is usually willing to continue working, even when tasks get harder later in training. Many people try to teach the entire behavior, or a large chunk of the behavior all at one time, rather than breaking it down. This practice is called *lumping*. Lumping may lead to frustration and failure if your dog cannot understand what is being asked of him. Teaching the performance of many agility obstacles and handling maneuvers can be most easily and effectively accomplished by *splitting*.

For many trainers, teaching reliable, independent weave pole performance is difficult. The desired finished product is the completion of 12 poles with a correct entry and no missed poles at full speed, regardless of handler position. Splitting weave pole training into its smallest parts might begin with setting up two weave poles and requiring the dog to go between those poles to get rewarded. The next requirement might be to go between the two poles with the first pole on the dog's left (a correct entry). Once the dog is doing well entering two poles on the correct side, the trainer might start altering her position for angled and off-side entries. Another requirement would include increasing the number of poles. Breaking down weave pole training into these smaller parts and teaching each part until it is a solid behavior will lead to the ultimate goal of the completion of 12 poles with a correct entry and no missed poles at full speed, regardless of handler position. Lumping together the requirements too soon can be frustrating and stressful for both dog and trainer.

GETTING BEHAVIORS – CLICKER STYLE

The first step in training is getting behaviors to happen. Once you get the behavior, you can then reinforce it (and it will increase in frequency). But, how do you get the behavior? In clicker training the three main ways of getting behaviors are shaping, luring, and targeting.

Shaping is a classic clicker training technique. In shaping, the trainer reinforces the dog (with a click and treat) for behaviors that lead in the direction of the desired behavior. The scientific term for this is *shaping by successive approximations*. The approximations should bring the dog closer and closer to the ultimate goal, often called the *target behavior*. In shaping, the dog is free to offer any behavior he likes; the trainer's job is to mark and reinforce those that will lead to the target behavior. The trainer does not direct the dog in any way. Shaping is about allowing the dog to think on his own and figure out what earns reinforcement.

For example, imagine that the target behavior is for your dog to get on the pause table. Using shaping, you would reinforce your dog for being in the vicinity of the table, for moving closer to the table, for looking at the table, for touching the table with his nose, for touching the table with his feet, and so on. At each step, you are requiring a behavior that moves closer and closer to the target.

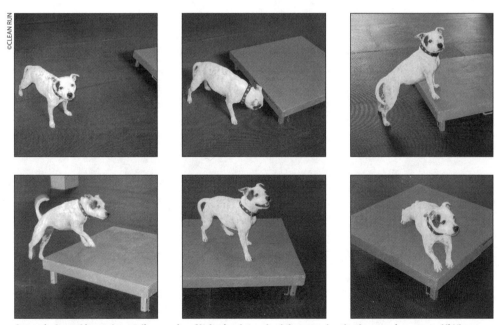

Successively marking and rewarding a series of behavioral steps leads here to a dog that learns to jump up and lie down on the pause table. Successful shaping requires learning how to balance keeping motivation high with demanding more complex behaviors.

The key to successful shaping is knowing how long to reinforce at a certain level and when to wait for more. This balancing act varies depending on the dog, the setting, and the target behavior. Shaping is definitely learned through hands-on experience. It's as much an art as a science. A trainer that is good at shaping has an almost instinctive awareness of when and how to move forward and when to wait for more from the dog. Practice shaping a variety of behaviors with different dogs to get a feel for it. Try simple behaviors at first, such as having your dog put his head on your knee, having him touch a particular object with his nose, or having him go to a specific spot in the room.

Luring is a much more familiar technique to many trainers. The lure is anything—typically held in the hand—that is used to entice the dog to follow. The theory is that the dog follows the lure and then learns to associate the accompanying hand motion with a desired behavior so that a lure is no longer necessary. The goal is to move the food to the end of the behavior as the reinforcer, rather than using it as a lure to cause the behavior. The hand motion becomes a signal. Then the trainer can simply reward the dog for performing the signaled behavior.

Typically, food lures are very effective, since most dogs will naturally follow food. A trainer can quickly and easily move a dog into desired positions using a food lure. Unfortunately, there are some common pitfalls associated with using a lure. For some dogs, the food lure becomes an overwhelming stimulus in the environment, and they do not pay attention to anything else. These dogs would follow the food lure off a cliff but have no idea that they are actually doing anything with their bodies. Such dogs learn to follow food, not to behave in any specific way. Another drawback with luring is that many people do not "fade" the lure systematically. Continual use of the lure leads to a dog that only responds when the lure is present. If the trainer suddenly removes the lure, the

Luring can be an effective way of "jump-starting" a behavior—getting it to happen quickly. Here the target behavior is getting the dog to put his front paws on the back of the chair. For most trainers, the greatest challenge with luring is fading the lure quickly enough so that the dog doesn't depend on its presence to offer the behavior.

dog does nothing. To avoid this problem the trainer must fade out the actual lure but keep using the same hand motion to get the dog to move. To accomplish this, the trainer alternates the use of the food lure with hand movement without the lure (empty hand trials). Once the dog moves as desired, the trainer marks and reinforces. Another potential problem with using food as a lure is that some dogs become very grabby and "sharky"—a painful and unpleasant situation for the trainer! Prior to training using food-luring, these dogs need to learn to take treats only when given permission, and always to take food gently.

Another effective way to get behaviors to happen is through the use of targeting. A target can be anything that the dog is taught to move towards and touch. Some common targets include plastic lids, paper plates, and the rubber grippers used to open jars. Food is never placed on the target since doing so would make the technique luring rather than targeting. Instead, the dog gets a mark and a treat after he has touched the target. Targeting is particularly useful in agility training, since it gets the dog to move away from the trainer. Many people use targeting to teach proper contact zone performance as well as for distance skills such as *Go on* (move ahead) and *Get out* (move away laterally).

Start target training up close, with the trainer holding the target in one hand. Mark and treat the dog for looking at the target, then for moving towards it, then for touching it with his nose, and so on. When the dog is reliably touching the target in the trainer's hand, the trainer can place the target on the floor and repeat the process. The goal is for the dog to move away from the trainer to the target, no matter where it is placed.

In general, clicker trainers avoid using physical manipulation (also known as modeling) to move the dog into position because putting your hands on the dog can have some unintended side effects in training. First, it may cause some dogs to become very passive and allow themselves to be modeled, but it doesn't teach them how to move in the desired ways on their own. Second, some dogs resist attempts to physically position or move them. This resistance will interfere with learning. Third, putting your hands on the dog often leads the dog to focus on you rather than on what he's doing. If we want dogs that are actively engaged in learning, hands-off training is often the best way to go.

CLICKER FUN

There are a few clicker games that encourage your dog to open up and experiment with new behaviors. This is good practice for any dog, but especially for one that is unsure or timid. As the trainer you will need to have plenty of patience while your dog figures out the "rules" of these games. For each game you'll need your clicker, lots of small, soft treats, and a quiet environment.

The classic game to introduce your dog to clicker training is 101 Things to Do with a Box. Its primary purpose is to teach your dog that you will reinforce him when *he* offers behaviors. This is a totally different experience for a dog that has been trained to wait to be told what to do. You can use any size or shape box for this exercise, but I like one big enough for the dog to sit in. As soon as you put the box in front of your dog, you need to be ready to click and treat any interest he shows in the box. Click your dog for looking at the box, for moving toward the box, for sniffing the box, for touching the box with a paw, and so on. At first, reinforce any behavior (including even the slightest glance toward the box) that involves the box. Be sure that you look at the box rather than your dog (keep your dog in your peripheral vision) and that you relax and smile while you wait for your dog to investigate the box. Keep your box sessions short (several minutes at most). Resist the urge to help your dog by throwing food in the box or pointing at the box. One purpose of this exercise is for your dog to discover that *offering behaviors will be reinforced*. Keep your clicks and treats coming as often as possible. Don't worry about getting a specific behavior; just reinforce any behavior that your dog offers.

While this game will teach your dog to open up and experiment with behaviors, it is a useful exercise for the trainer as well. It gives you an opportunity to practice your observation and timing. Watching and capturing small bits of behavior and clicking quickly and precisely are skills that need lots of hands-on experience. Because the results of this exercise don't matter to your dog's performance, it offers a great chance to work on improving your training abilities.

Once your dog has the basic idea, you can play 101 Things with any object. We've done it with chairs, leashes, jump bars on the ground, and so on. This activity will help a less outgoing or nervous dog become bolder and braver. It teaches him that he can control his environment because his actions make you click and treat. This builds confidence and makes training more enjoyable for the dog.

A more advanced variation on the box game is "Do Something Different." In this exercise, you reinforce creativity rather than repetition. Simply click and treat your dog for any behavior that is different from the last one you reinforced. It may take your dog a while to catch on to this concept, so be patient. Again, work in short sessions. Click any behavior at all, including moving ears, licking lips, wagging tail, looking in a different direction, and so on. This game will teach your dog that *trying something new during a training session will be rewarded.*

Teaching and practicing tricks is another way to help your dog (and you) have more fun while training. Again, tricks don't matter to your dog's eventual competition performance, so it's easier for trainers to practice their clicker skills without worrying about making mistakes. Many excellent trainers approach everything they teach their dogs with the attitude that "it's all tricks." If you adopt the attitude that every behavior you teach your dog is simply a trick, both you and your dog will relax and enjoy yourselves more. When teaching tricks you are limited only by your dog's physical abilities and your imagination. Spin, play dead, sit up, speak, back up, and so on, are just a few of the possibilities. A friend of ours taught her Belgian Sheepdog, Jedi, a trick a day until she ran out of ideas. Then she spent some time teaching her cat to do agility just for the fun of it. The cat ended up with good contact performance and better weave poles than some dogs! Remember, it's all tricks.

Once you have taught your dog a few tricks, you can then use them for warm-up, cool down, and as a way to FOCUS and connect with your dog in training.

Step One: Fun

Sabre's Story: Controlling the fun

Sabre was having a lot of fun doing agility his way. Unfortunately for Judy, his way didn't necessarily involve performing all the required obstacles. Our goal was for agility to continue to be fun but also to be accurate. When we started the FOCUS program, Sabre was only moderately food motivated. We needed to increase his  *interest in food reinforcers. Toys and play were highly motivating to Sabre, but they also sent him a bit over the edge. Using more food reinforcers helped him to settle down and concentrate on his job. Returning to Judy to collect his food reward also served to turn his attention more on her and less on the environment so she became more important to Sabre.*

WHY IS FUN THE FIRST STEP?

Agility is supposed to be fun! People often state that they—and their dogs— have fun doing agility. But for some, the fun aspect of agility doesn't come naturally, or it is lost along the way. Lack of confidence, performance anxiety, stress, and nervousness can affect both dogs and people and can ruin the fun.

If training is fun, then learning is easier for the dog. Fun lowers stress, and stress inhibits the learning process. It only makes sense that learning will be easier if you are relaxed and happy. Unfortunately, many people seem to have the misguided notion that fun and learning are mutually exclusive. They approach training as "serious business" that must be difficult to be effective. They also have some misguided notions about why the dog should work for the trainer. One of the most common is that the dog should do it simply "because I said so." This attitude suggests that the dog has no choice in the matter and that he should work because of the trainer's position of authority over him. This idea is wrong on both counts. First, dogs always have behavioral choices. While they may be pressured into performing (possibly to prevent the negative consequences of not performing), they may perform poorly and find ways to avoid working whenever possible.

Second, the trainer's authority must rely on power—either the power to reward or the power to punish. The dog doesn't respond correctly simply because he respects the trainer's position of authority. He responds correctly because he is either gaining reward or avoiding punishment. We have seen dogs complete agility courses correctly, but they are clearly not enjoying themselves. Extremely slow and careful, these dogs look as if they'd enjoy dental surgery more, and it is painful to watch them. Often these dogs have been punished for errors and now are working simply to avoid more punishment. A dog that is working to avoid punishment performs differently from a dog that is working to gain rewards.

Note: Sometimes slow and careful performances result from the dog having a soft and sensitive temperament rather than from the training approach. It is the trainer's responsibility, however, to change this performance by raising the dog's comfort and confidence level and making agility more fun for the dog.

Another common misconception is that using food, toys, and play in training is bribing the dog to work. A bribe is offered before a behavior has occurred, in an effort to get the behavior to happen. But used correctly, food, toys, and play are reinforcers supplied after desired behaviors and performances occur. Reinforcers are like a paycheck after the work has been completed. People work all week to earn their paychecks on Friday afternoon. They are not paid on Monday morning in the hope that they will then work all week. Most people would show up just long enough to pick up their paychecks; then they would be gone until the next payday. The same is true for dogs. Bribes are not effective training tools, but reinforcers are.

So, why does your dog work for you? There are two main possibilities: because it is enjoyable in and of itself (intrinsic motivation) or because of the external consequences (extrinsic motivation). You can think of the difference between the two types of motivation as the difference between a job and a hobby. Although people might enjoy aspects of their jobs, they don't do them for nothing. They are working for the external consequences (money, power, independence, status, benefits, and so on) that the job offers. This is extrinsic motivation. Most dogs work for the external reward as well. They may find some things they are asked to do in training enjoyable, but they need the positive consequences to keep them working happily and regularly. Hobbies, however, are different. People engage in hobbies simply because they enjoy the activity. Hobbies are reinforcing in and of themselves (intrinsic motivation) and don't require external rewards to maintain them. Some dogs find agility so rewarding on its own that they need little or no external reinforcement to maintain their enthusiasm. These dogs, mostly herding breeds, approach agility as a highly enjoyable activity and will perform simply for the pleasure of it. While this is a wonderful start, it's not enough to guarantee accurate and precise agility performances. Dogs that see agility as a hobby (or even an obsession!) need trainers who understand how to control the fun and keep the dog's attention on the handler when required.

In general, dogs that are extrinsically motivated will need more work on the fun aspects of the FOCUS program, while dogs that are intrinsically motivated will need more work on the obedience aspects. As training continues, however, you will need to balance both fun and obedience as required by the progress of the individual dog. Even the most intrinsically motivated dog will start to shut down and tune out the trainer if he isn't allowed to let loose and have fun on occasion. Control work isn't about constant drilling and suppressing all of the dog's natural enthusiasm. It is about using the dog's desire to work as the reward for exhibiting control.

The challenge for handlers of dogs that find agility self-rewarding is controlling the fun and keeping the dog's attention.

Bailing contacts may be more fun for a timid dog than drilling proper contact position, but making training fun does not mean that "anything goes." The handler's challenge is to find the balance that works between motivating and controlling the dog.

Making training fun for the extrinsically motivated dog does not mean a complete disregard for control and obedience. While the primary goal for a dog with little or no desire to perform agility is to raise his level of enjoyment, you should make agility fun in a structured and organized manner. Having fun doesn't mean "anything goes" and that the dog is not expected to respond to well-known and understood behaviors. Having fun is about instilling confidence and certainty so that the dog enjoys training and performing.

Making training fun is hard work! The trainer is responsible for controlling the dog's access to things that he will find fun and to providing those things when the dog exhibits desirable behaviors. Controlling the environment is a crucial factor in controlling the fun. If the dog can find ways to reward himself that don't involve the trainer, then he will see the trainer as irrelevant. Our job is to convince the dog that we are a vital part of his access to fun. This involves being aware of what the dog wants and finding ways to use his desire to get him to do something we want, a concept behaviorists call the *Premack Principle* or *Grandma's Law*. Grandma knew that you could increase vegetable consumption

IN FOCUS

Grandma's Law

In the 1960s David Premack confirmed what Grandma intuitively knew by performing a series of experiments with rats in which he discovered that high probability behavior could reinforce low probability behavior. Certain rats, he found, enjoyed running on their exercise wheel (a high probability behavior). He decided to make access to the wheel dependent on a lower probability behavior (drinking water). If the rats drank water, they were allowed to run on the exercise wheel. As expected, water drinking increased dramatically. Other rats enjoyed drinking water (a high probability behavior) more than running on the exercise wheel (a low probability behavior). He allowed these rats access to water only after running on the wheel. Again, as expected, the lower probability behavior (running on the wheel) increased dramatically.

The key to using the Premack principle effectively is in identifying a particular subject's high and low probability behaviors and making access to the preferred one dependent on the less preferred one. You need to discover what your dog prefers and use that as the reward for performing the less preferred behaviors. For example, Sabre's favorite obstacle is the tunnel. Judy asks him to perform the dogwalk (less preferred) and then allows him to barrel through a tunnel as his reward.

in children by making dessert contingent on eating vegetables. The Premack Principle—the scientific version of Grandma's Law—states that high probability behavior can increase low probability behavior. Grandma used the prospect of gobbling apple pie to get her grandchildren to choke down their peas. In this case then, eating dessert (a high probability behavior) increased eating vegetables (a low probability behavior). Likewise for dogs, if a high probability behavior is playing fetch and a low probability behavior is sitting, reinforcing sitting with fetching will increase how often the dog sits. The key is noticing these training opportunities on a daily basis and using them to their full advantage.

IDENTIFY THE FUN

To use fun effectively you must first identify the objects and activities that are fun for your dog. Think carefully and answer the following questions as completely as possible.

1. What are your dog's favorite foods? Rank them in terms of most to least desirable.
2. What are your dog's favorite toys? Rank them in terms of most to least desirable.
3. What games does your dog like to play? List those he plays both with people and with other dogs.
4. What are your dog's favorite activities? For example, go for a walk, take a ride in the car, chase squirrels, and so on.
5. What types of physical interaction does your dog enjoy? For example, roughhousing, belly-rubs, and so on.
6. What is your dog's biggest distraction when training? Note: this is often something he would find highly reinforcing if you could provide access to it.

Your answers to these questions should provide you with a list of rewards (reinforcers) to use both for training specific behaviors and for increasing your dog's enjoyment when working with you. Don't be stingy when using these rewards, but do be sure that they are controlled and used effectively either to reinforce desired behaviors or to change the dog's emotional state. We'll discuss how in the next pages.

MAKE THE FUN

Again, making training fun can be hard work! Increasing a dog's enthusiasm and motivation, and instilling a positive attitude toward training are the responsibility of the trainer. Some categories of rewards may be of low value to your dog at the moment or may only be effective in specific situations. Your job is to make the most of all the rewards that you have available by maximizing their value.

Food motivation

Food as a reinforcer can be a powerful tool, but many people report that their dogs are picky eaters or "don't like food." Believe us: we've heard them all when it comes to reasons why a dog won't work for food. But as we know, all dogs must

eat to survive. Food remains one of the best reinforcers we have available. If your dog is not food motivated, you need to work hard to change his attitude.

When we started the FOCUS program with Sabre, he was only mildly interested in food treats. He would much rather chase a ball as a reward. We started by

©DEBORAH JONES

using a new and highly desirable treat, chicken or turkey baby food, as a reinforcer. On the scale of food value where kibble is worth $1, baby food is usually worth $500. We used *click and lick* training to start. We asked Sabre for a behavior, which we clicked, and then allowed him a brief opportunity to lick some baby food right from the jar. Once we had his complete attention and interest, we could substitute other high-value treats for the baby food. Garlic chicken, string cheese, and Kix cereal turned out to be Sabre's favorites.

Food is useful as a reinforcer for several reasons. First, it is something we can carry and provide quickly and easily. Second, we can dole it out in small enough portions so that it is consumed within a few seconds yet the dog is not full. Even Deb's 4-pound Papillon can train for long periods using continual food rewards as long as they are small enough. Third, most dogs are naturally food motivated. Fourth, since we are going to feed the dog anyway, we might as well give him smaller portions in his bowl and use the rest to reinforce behaviors.

Start with hand-feeding. Hand-feeding is an important part of the FOCUS program. When the food comes from a bowl, the trainer is a secondary part of the feeding process. But when food comes from your hand, you are a much more obvious and important part of the process. In addition, hand-feeding allows you to require behaviors for each piece of food the dog is getting. We always recommend hand-feeding for the first few weeks with puppies as well as for the first few weeks that you are using the FOCUS program with an older dog. With puppies you can use hand-feeding as an opportunity to reinforce eye contact, to teach your puppy his name, and to instill a good recall cue (among many other things). With adult dogs you can also use hand-feeding to practice control behaviors (sit, down, wait, stay) and hand targeting, as well as to improve recall cues (more on these exercises in the "Obedience" section). You don't need to hand-feed the dog's entire meal to use it effectively. Just feeding the first 10 to 15 pieces of food this way, then presenting the rest of the food in a bowl, will be helpful.

Working for food increases its value. Food becomes more valuable and important when the dog must work to obtain it. Dogs do not appreciate "freebies" as much as those rewards they must earn. Using food as a reinforcer for behaviors turns it into a form of currency that the dog must work to gain. By requiring work for food, food motivation increases.

Choose your reinforcers thoughtfully. As we mentioned before, food reinforcers vary in their desirability and value. Some dogs find all treats valuable. Judy's older Sheltie, Morgan, works with same amount of enthusiasm whether the treat is kibble or liver. Other dogs have clear food preferences and will not work for what they consider a "low value" treat. Specific situations may call for a higher value food treat. For example, Sabre seemed incapable of concentrating on Judy while waiting their turn by the agility ring, especially when a fast dog was running. When she switched her reinforcer in that situation from Cheerios to turkey sausage, however, Sabre had no trouble at all concentrating on her.

Be prepared. Start thinking about food value and be prepared for those highly distracting situations by arming yourself with suitable food reinforcers. Rather than offering one treat that is rejected, then another, then another, start with the treat that you are 99% sure will work. Go into the situation armed with the "big guns" so that the probability of success (keeping your dog's focus) is high the first time. Once the desired behavior is solid, you can vary the value of your food reinforcer in that situation. One way to do this is to make up a "trail mix" that contains several different treats. You might have Cheerios, chicken, cheese, steak, and kibble all in one container. Grab a handful and use whichever one you randomly pick. The surprise of not knowing what the food reward will be keeps the dog interested and enthusiastic.

Fit the treat to the challenge. Sometimes it can be useful to designate specific foods only for certain behaviors or exercises. Saving a high-value food only for a specific behavior that is either being trained or retrained works well to keep the dog interested and keen to work. For initial weave pole training with her young dog Luna, Deb used baby food to keep motivation and attitude high. When she was first teaching her older Papillon Copper a recall in an open field, she used salmon only for that exercise (with excellent results). Fitting the food to the behavior/exercise/situation requires planning and thought prior to training.

Use jackpots judiciously. Using jackpots is another way to make food reinforcers highly effective tools. A jackpot is a special food reward. The distinguishing mark of a jackpot can be its high food value, large food quantity, or special delivery method. You can use a jackpot to mark an especially good effort, performance, or training breakthrough or to increase your dog's excitement level. For example,

if your dog has been struggling with weave poles and finally completes a nice set, you need to mark that moment (a clicker is great for this) and then provide a jackpot as a way of telling your dog "That was exactly what I wanted, and I will reward you well for weaving that way in the future!" It is heartbreaking to see a dog struggle and struggle and finally manage a breakthrough, only to have the trainer say *Good dog* and keep on going. Effort and struggle deserve extra reinforcement. Think of a jackpot as a bonus for hard work.

Many dogs have problems related to emotions rather than to behaviors. For example, a dog that is tense and nervous will be too internally focused and will not perform well. In this case a jackpot early in the training session, possibly given simply for moving out onto the training floor or field, will change the dog's internal state and help form a positive emotional association with training. We used a jackpot with Sabre at the end of his run to help maintain his positive emotions. Judy says that at the end of a run Sabre is like a kid who has just been told that Santa Claus isn't coming this year. His whole demeanor changes and he shuts down and goes flat. In this case, the special feature of the jackpot is in the way it is delivered. Judy makes up a combination of peanut butter, baby food, yogurt, diced chicken, and Cheerios and spreads that in the bottom and up the sides of a small plastic sandwich container. As soon as Sabre finishes his run, Judy starts talking to him about his jackpot as they walk from the ring to get it together. (Judy introduced Sabre to the word "jackpot" and the requirement of walking *with* Judy to get it in training first.) Then Judy allows Sabre to lick the jackpot from the container. Now Sabre leaves the ring as happily as he enters.

Make the effort to establish several foods as reinforcers for desired behaviors. It is much easier to train a dog that is motivated by food than one that is not. You will find that it is definitely worth the time and energy involved to build food motivation, and it pays off handsomely in your training.

Play and toy motivation

Agility is a fast-moving game. To play the game well the dog needs to be in the right state of physical and mental arousal. Too much and he will be "over the top" and out of control. Too little and he will be sluggish and disinterested. A moderate level of arousal is ideal both in training and in trialing. For the scientifically minded, the concept that a moderate level of arousal encourages learning is known as the Yerkes-Dodson law. One way to move your dog to the appropriate level (especially those in a low state of arousal) is by using play and toys.

Play energizes and excites. Yet play also requires a significant amount of involvement and energy from both dog and trainer. If you have a dog that doesn't seem to have much of a natural desire to play with you, it will take a bit of hard work to make play fun.

If you are starting with a puppy, be sure to play with him from the beginning. Most puppies are naturals at play, and this is the time to show him that you can be just as much fun as those of his own species. Often puppies and dogs that don't enjoy play have been inhibited by lack of confidence or fear. To play, a dog must relax, loosen up, and go with the flow. Introduce puppies to short, intense periods of play in all types of settings early in their lives.

In playing with your dog, you are establishing body language cues for arousal. Since agility, in large part, depends on your dog's ability to read your body language cues, play is actually a form of agility practice. If you're unsure how to engage your dog in play, take some time to watch dogs play with each other. Typically, dogs use multiple body language cues to communicate that they would like to play. A play bow (elbows on ground, rear end up in the air) is a classic gesture. Others include quickly darting toward and away from another dog, racing by another dog to encourage chasing, and lightly bumping into or jostling another dog from the side. You may also see dogs "play stalking" each other by moving forward low and slow, then pouncing and chasing. You can emulate these movements (to the best of your physical ability) to entice your dog to play with you.

While observing your dog interacting with other dogs, make note of his play preferences. Some dogs love to chase, while others like to be chased. Some dogs enjoy physical contact and wrestling. Some dogs like to play tug with other dogs, and some like to chase a moving object but lose interest when it is still.

©CLEAN RUN

Keep initial invitations to play light and subtle, especially with a sensitive or timid dog. Bold, expansive gestures and postures may scare or overwhelm him.

Don't be overwhelming when you start trying to entice your dog to play. Dogs read visual signals extremely well and subtle is better. Make tiny little play gestures, then back off a bit and see if you get a response. Moving away from your dog in play encourages him to move toward you. Dart in quickly, give your dog a playful tiny push on the shoulder, then quickly turn sideways and move away. Does your dog look alarmed or curious? If you haven't played much, keep your initial attempts low key and let your dog get used to this "new" you. Moving in toward your dog too much can be intimidating. Remember, play requires mutual cooperation and this is an *invitation* to play. You are asking your dog if he is interested, not insisting that he play or else.

Dogs that will play at home but not in public may be concerned about something in the environment, particularly the presence of other dogs, and may not feel comfortable letting down their guard and actively engaging in play. While many trainers will say you should insist that your dog play with you when, where, and how you want, it may be better to listen to what the dog is telling you in these situations and adjust your expectations. For example, Copper is a dog that is worried about the presence of other dogs, especially those that jump around and move unpredictably. At an agility trial he is busy monitoring the environment for danger, so he is completely uninterested in the toys that he loves at home and in training in familiar environments. Since Deb's job is to keep him safe and comfortable so that he can perform well, she does not insist that he play tug or chase in that setting. Instead, she uses high-value food rewards and practices tricks (spin, back up, speak, walk on your back legs, and so on) that he knows well. The movement excites and energizes him, success comes easily, and the food rewards keep him motivated. Insisting that he play in trial settings would only stress him and be counterproductive.

There are thousands of toys designed specifically for dogs. In addition, people are often creative in developing toys out of common household objects. As with play, the sooner you introduce your dog to different toys, the better. Also, using toys as reinforcers after a click or verbal marker gives you a wide variety of ways to reward your dog. If you use food exclusively in training, your dog will find toys a poor second choice in that situation. In the same respect, if you use toys exclusively in training, your dog will not see food as a desirable reinforcer. The goal is to have as many reinforcers available as possible.

50

Many agility trainers (and their dogs) enjoy the game of tug, and a variety of toys are designed specifically for this game. Tug is a great game for several reasons. It keeps the dog and handler actively engaged with each other so it helps develop FOCUS. It energizes the dog to prepare him for training and competition. At the end of a sequence or run it also serves as an outlet for excess energy. A quick game of tug is a good way to provide reinforcement during training, but there are a few things to keep in mind when playing this game.

Teach your dog to *Let go* on a verbal cue. While your dog is engaged in playing tug with you, pull out a high-value food treat and put it directly on your dog's nose. At the same time, move toward your dog to release the pressure on the toy, but don't let go of the toy. When your dog opens his mouth to take the treat, the toy will fall out. As soon as your dog takes the treat offer the toy and start tugging again. Repeat this often, adding the verbal cue *Out* as your dog opens his mouth to take the treat. Another good technique for getting your dog to voluntarily let go of a toy comes from obedience trainer Diane Carr. According to Diane, if your dog does not let go of the toy when you ask, you should move toward him and take his collar, holding him close to your body, and releasing the pressure on the toy. He can stand there and hold the toy, but you are not tugging any longer and you are restraining his movement. When he lets go of the toy, release his collar, praise him, and start the tugging game again.

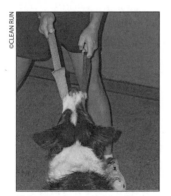  

If your dog does not let go when asked...

move toward him and take his collar and continue holding the toy. You have removed the element of fun. He'll be bored.

When the dog lets go of the toy, praise him and then release his collar and start the game again.

Only tug as hard as the dog does. Pulling and jerking with too much force can be unpleasant and painful for your dog. Gauge your pressure by the dog's pressure. Deb's 4-pound Papillon Luna loves to tug. But Deb needs to be careful not to jerk Luna off her feet or cause her to become airborne. In addition, tugging too much would probably loosen her little teeth.

Let the dog win at least half of the time. This rule goes against the old belief that the dog should never win, but think of how demotivating it would be to play a game that you always lose! This is especially true for those dogs that are not having enough fun already. Let them win, then pet and praise them while they still have the toy to build up their confidence. If your dog gets too aroused when playing tug (particularly if he nips or bites at you or jumps on you), then he needs to be kept at a calmer level during play. Play in shorter, less intense sessions, and be sure to instill a good *Out/Let Go* cue.

Some dogs will turn a game of Fetch into a game of Keep-away, and that means the dog is controlling the game.

Many dogs enjoy playing fetch. Fetch is a good game because it helps the dog to warm up and loosen up his muscles, takes the edge off after being cooped up on a long trial day, and encourages positive interaction between dog and trainer. While fetch has many advantages, it also has a few disadvantages.

Many times dogs will play Keep-away instead of Fetch. Teaching your dog to bring the object back to you so that you can throw it again may take some time and effort. One way to train a solid retrieve back to you is to play with two identical toys. Throw one for your dog and, as he turns back to you, show him the other and throw it in the opposite direction. He may decide to give up the one he has to chase the other one. This is a good place to use your marker—either verbal or clicker—and reward to teach your dog that returning the fetch toy earns him a reward and another throw (a double reward).

Another problem is that fetch takes the dog's focus off the handler, onto the toy, and out into the environment. A dog that has problems focusing needs to stay engaged with the handler rather than being encouraged to look out in the world for reinforcement. Modifying fetch to shorter distances or playing with a toy on a string or rope might be a better option for this type of dog.

If a dog enjoys playing fetch and reliably returns with the object, however, you can add fetch to your list of available reinforcers as well as using it for fun and exercise. With Sabre, Judy will often click and throw his ball rather than click and treat. Throwing the toy allows you to deliver your reinforcer at a distance. This is especially useful when you want to encourage movement and speed. Fetch is also a good way to reinforce static exercises such as start-line stays. You can lead out, click for a solid stay, and then throw the toy *behind* the dog as his reinforcer. This technique discourages forward movement during the stay, since the reinforcer will be delivered in the opposite direction.

During play you are discovering mutually enjoyable ways to interact with your dog. Loosen up, relax, and experiment. If you approach play as a serious training task, you will take all the fun out of it for both you and your dog. Play is part of the relationship foundation you are building with your dog. It needs to be encouraged and nurtured over time; it can't be forced or rushed. Dogs are perceptive creatures. If you are not truly enjoying your time spent playing with them, they will be aware of that fact.

TURNING THE DOG ON AND OFF

A critical element of the FOCUS program is the ability of the dog and trainer to engage with and disengage from each other quickly and easily. To make these switches, we need to introduce and teach our dogs arousal and relaxation cues. These cues are both words and actions that let the dog know what will happen next and what we expect from him.

The arousal cue tells the dog that he is now on *your time* and that you expect him to engage with you and work with you. This is the *on* switch. The relaxation cue tells the dog that he is now on *his time* and that he is free to chill out temporarily. This is the *off* switch. Clear and consistent use of these cues will help your dog to understand what is expected of him at any given time. It is not reasonable to expect your dog to always be on your time, especially if you are not 100% focused on your dog. Both of you must be intensely focused on each other when working together. You should introduce this intense focus in short segments since it can be exhausting for both dog and trainer.

The ON switch (arousal cues)

When you turn your dog on, you need to be 100% focused on him, and you expect him to maintain the same intensity of focus on you. You will be pairing specific, clear key words and phrases along with body language and movement, with this focus. The dog that is turned on should be energized, excited, and ready for activity.

Ready? Go!

Many trainers use the word *Ready?* as part of the dog's on switch. Using *Ready?* in a low, excited tone of voice while playing with your dog will help condition his emotional response to that word. You can play running games with your dog by lightly restraining him with your hand on his chest, asking him if he's *Ready? Ready? Ready?* until he is revved up, then pushing him back a bit while telling him *Go!* and running forward a few steps with him. You can pair the *Ready? Go!* phrase with chasing a toy by teasing your dog with the toy, asking him *Are you READY?*, then throwing the toy and encouraging him to *Go!* chase after it. Pair your dog's favorite toy with the *Ready?* cue by showing him the toy, teasing him with *Ready? Ready? Ready?*, and then playing tug with the toy.

You can also pair the *Ready? Go!* phrase with food by showing your dog a treat, teasing him a bit, asking him *Are you READY?*, then throwing the treat and encouraging him to *Go!* Another option is to toss a treat on the floor, restrain your dog by the chest, and ask him if he's *Ready?* When he's pulling to get to the treat, release him and command *Go!* All these games help make *Ready? Go!* an arousal cue.

Most dogs love playing the Two Treats game. Use treats that are easy to see on the floor and that roll easily. We prefer Planters Cheese Balls for big dogs and Kix cereal for small dogs. Show your dog the treat and tease him a bit asking *Ready? Ready?*, then roll the treat away from you to the side encouraging your dog to *Go!* As soon as your dog gets the treat and eats it, show him another one, use the *Ready?* cue and roll it in the opposite direction telling him to *Go!* Repeat this sequence sending the dog to chase a treat first in one direction, then the other. This game is a good warm-up exercise. It gets most dogs energized and excited.

Using the Ready? Go! cue to invite chasing food in the Two Treats game is guaranteed to get most dogs active, energized, and ready to work.

Smile and spit

Competition obedience trainers have developed a food delivery technique that some may find unusual (or even disgusting) but that works very well. Rather than handing the dog a treat or dropping it, they spit the food at the dog. This method serves to keep the dog focused on the handler's face. It is important to practice a bit first, so that your dog understands that he can catch the food that drops from your mouth. Start close to your dog, show him the food, put it in your mouth, point at your mouth, and spit it toward your dog's face. There is definitely a learning curve for both dog and trainer with this method! At first, Deb's Papillon Copper simply closed his eyes when he saw food dropping toward his face. Your food choice for this method makes a big difference in how well and how easily the process works. It has to be something the trainer is willing to put in her mouth and that is neither too dry nor gets mushy. Small bits of cheese, pieces of chicken, and/or micro-waved hotdog bits work well.

This food delivery technique works well with the FOCUS program because it allows you to carry your food reinforcer in a non-obvious place and to surprise your dog with a great reward when he offers attention. In addition, you can pair a fairly common signal, your smile, with the delivery of food. This is why we call it the *smile and spit* technique. Simply smile before you spit food to your dog. He will learn that looking at your face pays off, and that seeing you smile is a signal that good things are coming.

Body language and movement

Your body language and movement can also be an arousal cue for your dog. Besides the verbal cue, adopting a body posture that is playful and appealing to your dog will help to get your dog excited and ready to engage with you. Many dogs will respond with interest if you suddenly freeze, crouch a bit, hunch your shoulders slightly, and quickly dart first toward and then away from your dog. If your dog is comfortable with more physical play you might reach out and lightly pinch your dog's shoulder or hip before you dart away. Or give your dog a playful little shove. Whatever your physical movement, keep it non-threatening and inviting. Experiment to see what your dog will respond to with curiosity and then build on that.

Chase games can be good ways to increase your dog's level of excitement and arousal. Use your verbal arousal cue, then either chase your dog or encourage him to chase you (based on his play preference). Copper loves to be chased and Deb uses this game, along with lightly pinching his rear end and telling him "I'm gonna get you!" while she chases him. A different dog might prefer chasing you.

After using your verbal arousal cue you might run a short distance encouraging your dog with *Let's go!* Then praise him lavishly for chasing and "catching" you.

Speak!

Teaching your dog to *Speak* on cue can be a way to bring a more inhibited dog out of his shell. A little bit of excited barking can bring a dog's attitude up and make him feel energized. Be careful, however, because barking is such an intrinsically enjoyable activity, a dog could take it to an extreme if not carefully monitored. The easiest way to teach your dog to speak is to find a stimulus that naturally elicits the response. It may be a doorbell, for example. You could have someone ring the doorbell, and when your dog barks mark the sound and reward it. Or you could find something that gets your dog mildly frustrated. Many dogs, when frustrated, will naturally make noises. Deb taught her Labrador Retriever, Katie, to bark by simply holding Katie's food bowl until she made some noise, then reinforcing sounds by feeding. Mark and reward any sounds at first. Katie started with whimpering, then whining, then yipping, before moving into barking. Once she was barking regularly, Deb added a verbal command and a hand signal to cue the behavior.

Touch, Spin, and Get back

Getting your dog up and moving is another way to encourage arousal. You can teach some simple behaviors to get him moving. Once you have taught your dog to touch your hand (described in the "Stationary Control" section), you can use this movement to encourage him to jump up and touch your hand. Start by holding your hand low enough so your dog only needs to stretch his neck and head slightly to reach it. When he touches your hand, mark and reward the behavior. Then move your hand to a different spot and ask for the behavior again. As your dog is successful, you can raise your hand higher and higher, until his front feet must come up off the ground to touch your palm. Eventually, your dog can learn to leap up in the air to touch your hand. Be careful about your dog's footing when practicing this exercise. You don't want him to slip and fall.

You can also teach your dog to make tight circles, nose to tail, as a way to get him energized and excited. It is easy to encourage a dog to spin by luring him with a treat held at his nose height. Mark and reward your dog for moving in the desired direction. It's best to start with one direction and train that completely first, then train the other direction. Use different verbal cues for each. Judy uses *Spin* when Sabre circles to his left and *Twist* when he circles to his right.

Many dogs get energized and excited by turning in tight circles, a behavior that is easily taught using a lure at the dog's nose height.

Another physical skill that can also serve as a way to get your dog animated and excited is teaching your dog to back up. Your dog will learn to stand facing you and to move straight back away from you. There are several ways to teach this behavior. You could use physical prompting by moving toward your dog. As he backs up to get out of your way you can mark and reward that movement. Or you could approach training your dog to back up as a shaping exercise, waiting for your dog to offer the behavior, and then marking and reinforcing each time your dog moves his body away from you. Remember to shape in tiny steps, looking for lifting a single paw to start. You could also teach backing up by luring the dog with a treat. If you place the treat under the dog's chin and move it slowly toward his chest, he should put his head down and move backwards to try to follow it. You can then mark this behavior. With some training and practice many dogs can learn to back up for quite a distance. They seem to enjoy practicing this skill.

Adding a behavior

When you are first teaching arousal cues you should use the cues, then work to get your dog in an animated and excited state using any of the ideas or techniques mentioned above. Start with short sessions (about 30 seconds). You can move to longer periods of sustained and intense interaction as your dog is able to concentrate on you and your shared activity. Once your dog reliably responds with animation and excitement to your arousal cues, you can start adding in a work requirement: First give your arousal cues, and then ask your dog for a well-known and practiced behavior. When your dog responds correctly, you can use a verbal marker (such as *Yes!*) then play with your dog or let him chase after some treats you toss. The entire sequence (arousal cues, behavior request, behavior, and reinforcement) should take no more than 30 seconds.

The OFF switch (relaxation cues)

Teaching your dog that it's okay to relax for a while is as important as teaching him to engage with you. Your dog cannot maintain an extremely high level of engagement for long periods of time. Being highly focused and concentrating is both physically and mentally exhausting. You may remember how you needed some time to relax and clear your head after taking a difficult test in school. Your dog will have a similar response. He needs to be given frequent breaks to regroup and calm down. Likewise, if you are training and you will be concentrating on the course, your instructor, or on another dog and handler instead of your own dog, you should turn your dog off to let him relax until it's time to work again. Again, you will use verbal and physical cues to tell your dog that you are done interacting with each other for the moment and that he is back on *his* time. This is the off switch.

When he is off, you are giving him permission to move to a less vigilant state, but he is not completely "off the clock" (equivalent to the military's *Dismissed*). During a training session, the off condition functions as a standby mode akin to the military's command *At ease*. Your dog needs to learn that he can relax, observe the environment, and take any position (sit, stand, down) that is comfortable for him, but he may be called back into action at any time. This makes the off condition different from times when the dog is not working at all and can just "be a dog." In those cases, the dog has "clocked out" and will not be interacting with you in training for a longer time. In these situations, you may want to put your dog in an ex-pen or crate to allow him to relax completely.

Many trainers use the verbal cue *OK* as a release word to cue the dog that he has finished an exercise and is done performing for the moment. In addition, they often follow *OK* with rewards such as treats and play, so rather than making *OK* a relaxation cue, this practice accomplishes the opposite. Pairing *OK* with exciting events makes it an arousal cue instead, as anyone who has watched the stay exercises during an obedience competition has seen. After the long sit exercise, handlers return to their dogs and release them with great enthusiasm and excitement. The dogs usually jump up, happy and energized, since the release has usually been paired with rewards. The handlers then immediately ask their dogs to settle into the long down exercise. It is difficult for some dogs to make this transition back into a quieter physical and emotional state.

In the FOCUS program, the relaxation cue means that the handler is no longer going to be interacting with or reinforcing the dog for a period of time. This gives the dog a chance to readjust his emotional state from excited to calm. Making the relaxation cue low-key teaches the dog that the "good stuff" (training) is

©DIANELEWISPHOTOGRAPHY.COM

In the OFF mode, a dog relaxes comfortably "at ease."

finished for the moment. Dogs should learn that the relaxation cue is a slightly unhappy event, since it means that no more rewards will be available in the short-term. Finishing an exercise or training session should be much less enjoyable than being engaged in one.

You can also use your body language to tell your dog that you are no longer working with him. Stand up straight rather than bending into your dog, turn your shoulders slightly away from him, break off eye contact, and gaze slightly past him rather than at him. You might also shift your weight slightly to one side or the other. Pairing this change in posture and eye contact with your verbal relaxation cue will help your dog understand that the intense interaction between the two of you is over for the moment.

When you first start using your arousal and relaxation cues, you can help your dog understand the difference by quietly reinforcing calm behavior after your dog has been turned off. Frequent feeding of small, soft treats in a quiet and calm manner will help your dog to move to a more relaxed internal state. You are not marking and rewarding any specific behavior here. You are simply feeding as a way to keep your dog calm and relaxed. All your movements should be slow and gentle. As long as your dog stays quiet, you will provide slow, constant feeding.

It helps many dogs to have a more specific task than to simply chill out when they are off. Teaching your dog to go to and stay on a rug or mat can be useful for those times when the dog is not expected to be working. A rug or mat is easy to carry with you wherever you go and can serve as a visual cue for your dog that he can relax and take it easy. To start, set out the mat and mark and reward your dog each time he approaches or puts a foot on the mat. Gradually raise your requirements for reinforcement to having two feet on the mat, then three, then all four before you will mark and reward. Once your dog keeps all his feet on the mat, you can add a sit as a requirement for reward. Eventually, the goal would be for your dog to maintain a relaxed down-stay on the mat whenever he is given the opportunity. If you practice in short training sessions, your dog will get the idea quickly. Take the mat to several different places to help your dog understand that he should go to and stay on the mat in all situations.

The Crazy Dog Game helps your dog practice switching quickly and easily between active engagement and relaxation, a skill he'll need in agility.

Once your dog understands *on* and *off* cues, you can practice them by playing the Crazy Dog Game. In this game you will turn your dog on using his arousal cues, work him up into a high state of excitement, and then turn him off using his relaxation cues. This game teaches your dog to move from an emotional high back to a calmer state, and then back to a high state of excitement again. To have a solid performance in agility, it is necessary for your dog to become comfortable with rapid changes in his emotional state. The Crazy Dog Game is a way of practicing for those rapid changes. To start, turn your dog on with words, play, movement—whatever works to get him excited. When he is totally up and engaged in playing with you, turn your dog off with his relaxation word and changes in your body language. Stop all movement and interaction with your dog, break off eye contact, and go completely still. Wait until your dog settles down and relaxes, then turn him on again. Repeat this process several times. As you practice, the amount of time your dog is on should increase, and the amount of time it takes him to turn off should decrease. Your dog should be able to remain actively engaged with you for longer and longer periods of time without losing focus because he will become more aware of your cues and body language and begin responding to you much more quickly.

STRESS KILLS FUN

Many times a dog is not having fun because he is nervous, worried, or anxious. These unpleasant emotions can have any number of causes including confusion, fear, a bad experience, or an overload of information. Perhaps the dog can perform the requested behaviors in certain situations (such as during training), but in other situations (such as at a trial) his negative emotional state interferes. In cases like this, it is essential to address the emotional issues to improve performance.

When considering the effects of stress and other emotional issues it is necessary to understand the basic difference between classical and operant conditioning. Most dog training uses operant conditioning, controlling the consequences of the dog's behavior. Providing reinforcement for desired behaviors is a prime example of using operant conditioning. The dog learns that what he does has a direct effect on the outcome. Classical conditioning, on the other hand, is the learning process that occurs when something in the environment triggers an emotional response. Animals and people learn relationships between stimuli (external objects or events) and automatic responses—including most fears and phobias—through the process of classical conditioning. For example, many people are afraid of spiders although most spiders are harmless. Some people, however, have an intense fear and avoidance response to any spider. They have learned this exaggerated reaction so that now the stimulus (spider) automatically evokes the response (fear and avoidance). This process can occur between nearly any stimulus and any response. If your dog took a bad fall off the dogwalk, for example, he may develop a fear and avoidance response to the dogwalk. If not handled properly, the fear and avoidance response will escalate.

If your dog has developed a negative emotional reaction to agility in general or to a specific agility obstacle, there are ways to make things better. While a discussion of these techniques would require an entire book of its own, we will give you a few ideas here. If your dog has just had a bad experience with a particular piece of equipment, it is important to follow the *24-Hour Rule*. As difficult as it may be, it is best to do nothing related to that piece of equipment for 24 hours.

A flattened profile and claws desperately clinging to the sides of the seesaw show a stressed, fearful dog. Trialing under these circumstances will further deflate the dog's confidence and increase the dog's fear of the teeter.

Most trainers want to fix the problem immediately by getting the dog back on the obstacle as soon as possible. They mistakenly believe that getting the dog on the obstacle "one more time" will magically make the problem disappear. Unfortunately, the dog is usually in a negative emotional state at that moment, and any repeated exposure to the stimulus (the obstacle) simply strengthens the dog's belief that he should be afraid.

After at least 24 hours have passed, you can introduce the dog to the obstacle again, but be prepared to reinforce extremely highly for any interaction with the obstacle at all. Rather than asking your dog to perform the entire behavior associated with the equipment, go back to marking and rewarding looking at, moving toward, or putting a foot on the obstacle. Over several short training sessions move back to requiring more from the dog. Going back to basics with an obstacle will *never* hurt. It will help your dog develop confidence again. Removing the pressure to perform will keep your dog from developing an avoidance response to the obstacle. If you are entered in a trial and your dog is having difficulty with an obstacle, don't push your dog to perform that obstacle. If he decides to avoid it and run by, just let it go and move on. Work on getting the behavior back in training first.

©CLEAN RUN

Playing in a trial setting can help a stressed or an overexcited dog relax.

Some dogs display a negative emotional response to the trial situation itself. Several stimuli in the environment may trigger this response. The excitement of the situation, the trainer's increased level of nervousness, the number of other dogs, and so on—all can cue fear and anxiety in the dog. This dog may be perfectly comfortable when training in familiar environments but may freeze up and be unable to perform well at a trial. The way to work through this problem is to lower the dog's stress level by lowering your expectations for his performance. It may be beneficial to simply take the dog to trials without entering him, to allow him to experience the show environment without added pressure or stress.

You will also need to provide extremely high-value rewards to help move your dog to a more relaxed internal state. These rewards are not related to your dog's behavior; rather, you give them to help your dog maintain the desired emotional state. Fairly constant feeding of small, soft treats helps to keep the dog calm and relaxed. The only requirement for getting rewards is that your dog remains calm.

A repertoire of "silly pet tricks" that your dog enjoys performing can relax and focus both of you as you wait your turn to go in the ring.

He doesn't have to do anything else to earn them.

When you ask your dog for specific behaviors at a trial site, using jackpots can help keep him feeling positively about the situation. In a trial setting ask your dog for simple, well-known behaviors and reinforce him highly for performing those. Your dog needs to be able to change his focus from his unpleasant internal state to behaviors he can perform successfully. Even though the behaviors you ask for would be easy for your dog in most situations, you want him to learn that doing them at a trial pays off really well.

Dogs can develop a tolerance for stress if you increase the stress level slowly over time. This is the same principle as giving a flu vaccination. Being exposed to a small dose of the virus stimulates the body to produce protective antibodies against future exposure. This same basic process also works to increase a dog's ability to withstand stressful events. Introducing small stressors in controlled settings will give your dog the opportunity to learn how to adjust and deal with bigger stressors in the future. The key to success with this technique is increasing stress levels only when your dog is coping well at the existing level. Throwing too much too soon at your dog will lead to fear, anxiety, and failure.

Early in their agility careers, some dogs are exposed to high levels of stress at their first trials. Such high stress could be due to changes in the environment, handler nerves, or simply a lack of ring experience. Whatever the cause, the dog begins associating stress and anxiety with trial situations. Sometimes the handler gets tense and excited and puts much more pressure on the dog to perform at trials than in training. Even if the dog qualifies in this situation, there may be long-term damage to his enthusiasm and attitude about showing. If a dog is to have a long and successful agility career, it is much more important to consider his emotional state and confidence level in the beginning than to be concerned about perfect performance. It is especially important in the early stages of the dog's career that the handler does not let frustration or anxiety because of performance errors affect the dog. Perfect performance comes with confidence and positive experience.

ORGANIZED FUN

To increase the fun for your dog you need to work on the following aspects of the FOCUS program:

1. Establish and use a variety of food reinforcers.

2. Hand-feed for at least two weeks.

3. Introduce a clear and positive communication and reinforcement system (such as clicker training).

4. Work hard at play! Find toys and games that your dog enjoys and use them in many settings.

5. Develop on and off switches for your dog. Find ways to increase and decrease your dog's arousal level.

6. Monitor your dog's stress level. Be aware of your dog's emotions and how these may influence training and performance.

Step Two: Obedience

Sabre's Story: We don't need no stinkin' obedience!

Judy thought that Sabre would magically become more responsive and obedient as he matured. She also thought that too much strict obedience training would decrease his drive and ruin his enthusiasm. Certainly teaching obedience in a force-based, coercive manner could dampen Sabre's high spirits. Using positive techniques, such as  clicker training, however, can make obedience exercises fun and interesting and open a line of clear communication between dog and trainer. As driven as Sabre is, he pays much more attention now than when he was running wild and free. He even enjoys doing his start-line and table stays.*

WHY IS OBEDIENCE NECESSARY?

It's agility! Why do we need to do that boring obedience stuff? Isn't it all about running, jumping, playing, and having fun?

Obedience is *not* a bad word. When we speak of obedience in this book, we are not talking about traditional, force-based methods. We are also not talking about highly practiced, technically precise, choreographed movements. Instead, we are referring to the use of positively based, highly motivational methods to teach the behaviors, skills, and abilities necessary for successful agility performance. We will discuss techniques for teaching these behaviors and skills in the upcoming section, "Control Exercises."

Many people have a negative view of obedience training as an overly restrictive and demotivating process for the dog. Many agility trainers are concerned about how to maintain the dog's enthusiasm and drive while gaining control of his behavior. They worry that a structured obedience program will ruin the dog's enjoyment of agility and undermine his confidence. The good news is that obedience and agility are *not* mutually exclusive (if both are taught in a positive manner). Rather than slowing the dog down and undermining his confidence, reinforcement-based obedience training increases the dog's (and the handler's) enjoyment of the game. The dog learns the rules that lead to his rewards, and the handler gets more consistent and faster performances from the dog. As discussed earlier, the dog learns that certain behaviors predictably lead to certain outcomes. Once he understands this basic concept, he is ready to learn specific behaviors and activities.

Agility dogs need a good, solid obedience foundation, ideally before they start agility training. It is a mistake to move too quickly in agility and let the dog have his head on the course, allowing him to run wild and free before the handler has good verbal control. Giving the dog this much uncontrolled freedom too soon leads to a dog that enjoys the adrenaline rush of agility but doesn't understand the teamwork aspect. It will take much remedial work to convince this dog that listening to his handler is necessary in agility.

If we do our foundation work in obedience first, we will have a dog that quickly and correctly responds to cues and signals. Laying a strong obedience foundation initially is much easier than trying to add it later. It is possible, however, to go back at any time in the dog's agility career to fix unwanted behaviors, gain more control, and instill a positive attitude toward obedience. But keep in mind that fixing pre-existing control problems requires considerably more effort and dedication than if you simply had dealt with the problem correctly in the beginning.

Clearly, dogs that are out of control need more obedience work, but even soft, sensitive dogs require an obedience foundation to perform to their full potential in agility. Obedience can instill confidence by making interactions and situations clear and understandable for the dog. If the dog knows how to respond correctly and to earn rewards, he will be much more sure of himself. This confidence will lead to faster and more accurate performances.

With practice, a dog that clearly understands the relationship between his behavior and the consequences will respond more and more swiftly. Rapid responses are essential in agility, since speed is an element of success. Accurate but slow performances may qualify at the lower levels of competition, but at the highest levels, speed is often critical (especially for those who want to be competitive). Encouraging quick responses to obedience cues and signals from the beginning is vital for successful agility performances.

Control and obedience start in the real world, long before you hit the agility field. By controlling your dog's access to the resources in the environment, you place yourself in a position of power. One of the most important lessons your dog can learn is that he needs to come to you for anything and everything that he wants. Allowing your dog to find his own fun and reinforcement in the environment will undermine control work. Keep yourself at the center of all your dog's activities. Make him work to earn his rewards, including interaction with other dogs and access to fun activities like a run in the park.

Learning doesn't end when you leave class or end a training session. Learning is continuous: it goes on every moment of the day. Whether you intend to teach your dog something doesn't matter: learning is always happening. If you are working hard at teaching your dog control in agility, then you will need to be aware of his control issues at home as well. There needs to be consistency between your expectations in formal training sessions and your expectations of your dog's behavior in real life. For example, a student of Deb's spent a class session working on control exercises, particularly walking politely. As the student and her dog left the building, Deb saw the dog pulling the student to the car. This inconsistency makes learning much more difficult for the dog.

CONTROL EXERCISES

You can teach these control exercises long before you introduce your puppy or dog to agility equipment. Start each exercise in a quiet, calm environment and then move to increasingly distracting situations as your dog demonstrates his understanding of the behaviors. Bring out the high-value treats when you need to be more interesting than anything else in the environment. On the following pages, we outline the fundamental control exercises in the FOCUS program and suggest techniques for teaching them.

STATIONARY CONTROL

For all these exercises the trainer is stationary, even though the dog is moving in the recall and hand targeting. We use the term *stationary* to distinguish these from the more advanced moving control exercises where dog and trainer move together.

Look at me: The easiest and most effective way to teach your dog to look at you more often is to reinforce him whenever he offers you any attention. Be prepared to mark the desired behavior using either a word or a click. Have your treats handy so you don't miss any opportunities. Rather than asking for attention, you will be waiting for your dog to glance in your direction, then capturing that glance with a marker and rewarding it with a treat. If you don't have treats handy, you should still acknowledge your dog's attention with praise, petting, and play. If looking at you is reinforced, it will increase in frequency.

Hand target: Teaching your dog to move toward and touch your open palm is an important foundation exercise in agility. It allows you to bring your dog in close to you as needed. Simply hold your palm at your dog's eye level, then mark and treat for any movement toward your hand. Your eventual goal is to have your dog move toward and touch your hand no matter where you hold it. In the beginning, however, you are simply looking for him to show interest in your hand and rewarding that interest. As you progress you will withhold the mark and treat until your dog moves toward your hand, then actually touches your hand with his nose. Raise your requirements in small, gradual increments over several training sessions.

Recall: For initial recall training we suggest beginning with *in your face* recalls. Start by facing and standing directly in front of your dog. Say your dog's name, give your recall cue (*Here, Come, With me,* and so on), then immediately mark and treat. Your dog does *not* have to do anything except take the treats offered to him. This exercise sets your dog up for guaranteed success because he cannot make a mistake. The purpose of this exercise is for your dog to form a highly positive association with his recall cue. Practice this exercise in as many different situations as possible.

The next step in your recall training would be the Go/Come Game. In this game you get your dog to *Go* by rolling a small round treat on the floor 2' to 3' feet in front of you and encouraging your dog to chase and eat it. As soon as your dog swallows the treat, call your dog using his name and recall cue, then use a marker as he turns toward you, and treat when he comes back to you. As your dog begins to understand this game withhold the click until your dog is moving toward you. Delay the marker a bit longer as your training progresses, so that you are then using the behavioral marker when the dog actually gets to you.

How to Build a Behavior

This is a general guide for building new behaviors. The steps listed may need to be revised or modified for specific situations but tend to serve as a good overall model.

1. Get the behavior. There are a number of ways to get any particular behavior, or part of a behavior, to occur. The best way to get a behavior depends on the individual dog, the situation, and the desired behavior. Shaping, luring, and/or targeting are good ways to build behaviors. If possible it is generally best to avoid using physical manipulation.

2. Reinforce the behavior. As soon as the behavior occurs, reinforce it so it will be repeated. We feel that using a clicker is the best way to mark the desired behavior. Follow each click with a treat, toy, or play, depending on the particular dog. Continue at this step until the dog is regularly and quickly repeating the desired behavior when given the opportunity.

3. Fade the lure or target. If you used luring or targeting to initially cause the behavior, you must fade the lure or target. Fading should be gradual and systematic over several trials.

4. Raise the criteria as the dog progresses. Three possible criteria for any behavior are duration, distance, and distraction. Typically, the criteria are added in that order. Each criterion must be raised separately from the others and then combined as the dog becomes confident in performing the desired behavior (see "Shifting Criteria," page 76)

5. Add a verbal cue. Once the dog is performing the desired behavior reliably with speed, with the required criteria, you should add a verbal cue just before the behavior occurs. The same holds for any hand signals or body language cues (see "Adding Cues and Signals," page 72).

6. Vary the reinforcement schedule. Increase the requirements for reinforcement. Ask for two or three repetitions of a well-known behavior before reinforcing. To keep your dog working, it's important to be unpredictable in your reinforcement schedule. Sometimes reinforce two behaviors in a row; other times ask for three or four before reinforcing (see "Varying the Reinforcement Schedule," page 80).

7. Help your dog generalize. Practice the behavior (or an easier form of the behavior) in many different settings. A dog will perform a truly generalized behavior, on cue, in any situation. This kind of reliability requires repeated practice in a variety of locations.

©CLEAN RUN

Sit: You can teach a sit fairly quickly by using a food lure. Place the food almost directly on your dog's nose and move it up and at a slight angle (away from the dog and towards you). Your dog's nose should follow the food and he should tuck his hind legs under him as he sits. (If you angle the food back above the dog's head toward his ears, he will rock back on his haunches. Rocking back on the haunches may be of no consequence for agility but has implications for obedience competition, because a dog that rocks back is way out of heel position, or too far away on a front.) Then mark and give your dog his treat. After luring a few times, try using the same hand motion without the lure to entice your dog to move into the sit. Most dogs will still follow your hand even without the food. Then you can mark and treat following the sit.

Down: You can teach a down fairly quickly using a food lure. There are two ways that a dog can move into the down position. First, from a sitting position, the dog can move his front legs forward and lower himself to the ground. Second, from a standing position, the dog folds back, collapsing into a down, with no sit required. Referred to variously as the *fold-back, sphinx,* or *accordion* down, this is the preferred down in performance dogs since the dog can drop into and pop out of this position quickly.

Starting with the dog in a stand, move a food lure from his nose to the middle of his chest, slightly into the dog and toward the ground. Your luring should cause the dog to lower his head. Mark and treat this head movement. Repeat several times. The next step is to move the lure further toward the ground so that, in addition to lowering his head, the dog also folds his front legs back and his elbows touch the ground. Continue moving the food lure toward the ground, and wait to mark until the dog bends his elbows. Repeat this step several times. Finally, once the dog's head and elbows are on the ground, move the food lure up slightly. This should cause the dog to drop his rear end as well. Mark and treat when the dog's rear end hits the ground.

Get the head down: Lure standing dog to lower head by following treat toward ground.

Get the front end down: As the lure gets closer to the ground, the the dog will have to lower his whole front end until he is forced to fold his elbows on the ground. This stage will look like a play-bow.

Get the rear end down: Once you've got the front end down, raise the lure slightly so the dog has to look up. That'll make him drop his rear.

Note: The fold-back down enables the dog to instantly drop from and rise to a stand because it doesn't require him to reshuffle his front feet. Downing a dog from a sit requires that you get the dog to move his forelegs forward, basically "walking" into a down. Once a dog learns the fold-back down, dropping and rising become a one-step process so are quicker.

The dog in the top image is in the correct "close" position while in the second image, he is out of position. He has swung around in front of his trainer and will cross her path and trip her up if they continue forward.

Close (left side) and Side (right side): Teaching your dog to come into your side facing the same direction that you are and to maintain that position is vitally important for keeping control. Your dog needs to learn to come to the desired side of your body and to stay there until released. Your dog can either sit or stand at your side, but he must make eye contact with you in this position. The eye contact gives you a connection to your dog. If you have already taught your dog to target your hand, you can use your hand to bring him into position next to you. Mark and treat when your dog is beside you and facing the same direction that you are. For this exercise be sure that your dog is not in front of you when he gets the treat. Dogs tend to gravitate to the spot where they receive treats. So, if you want your dog to move into and stay at your side, you need to provide the treats in that position. If your dog does not target your hand yet, you can teach this exercise using a food lure instead. Teach each side separately. Start with one and train until your dog quickly and easily moves into that position before training the other side.

Wait and Stay: Although many trainers use the cues *Wait* and *Stay* interchangeably, others make a clear distinction between these two. We use *Wait* to mean "Hold still, but be ready since you will be receiving another cue soon." On the other hand, *Stay* means "Do not move out of position until I formally release you." Whatever you decide, use your cues consistently. Throughout this section we use the term *Stay* for simplicity.

Being still can be difficult for many dogs. High-drive dogs have a hard time turning down the adrenaline enough to inhibit action whereas less confident dogs may be worried about what might happen to them when their owners leave and they are instructed not to move. A positively trained stay can work for both types of dogs. It gives high-drive dogs the motivation to hold still, and it gives less confident dogs a feeling of security.

Adding Cues and Signals

Obedience teaches the dog to respond to handler cues and signals. This is what behaviorists call stimulus control. A stimulus is something that precedes (comes before) and elicits (causes) a behavior. For example, a running squirrel is a stimulus that brings out the chase response. In many dogs this is an innate response, an inborn behavior pattern. A dog that has been trained to respond to the *Come* cue by moving toward you operates under stimulus control when he responds to the cue. This response is not innate, however; it must be taught. An agility dog that is under good stimulus control will respond quickly and correctly to handler cues for direction and obstacle performance. This control leads to a much higher probability of correct and successful agility runs.

When adding a verbal cue to a behavior, it is important to wait until the dog is performing the behavior regularly, correctly, and swiftly when given the opportunity. Using a verbal cue too soon can lead to problems with stimulus control. For example, Sabre used to be antsy when left on a start-line stay; he would fidget and scoot. Judy was using the verbal cue *Stay* for this behavior. By constantly connecting the verbal cue with an imperfect behavior, Judy had inadvertently taught Sabre that *Stay* meant to fidget and scoot rather than to hold still. To solve this problem we had to retrain the behavior from the ground up and use a different verbal cue. We re-taught the sit and simply used the cue *Sit* to mean "continue sitting until released." Similarly, if you add a cue before the dog offers the behavior quickly and with

©DALE RUFF

gusto, then you run the risk of getting a solid but slow response to the cue. That's not what you want in the fast-paced sport of agility.

When introducing a verbal cue, you should add it just as you see the dog beginning to perform the desired behavior. At first, the cue is simply telling the dog what he is already doing. As you continue training, you move the cue ahead until it occurs before the behavior.

There may be times when you want to change the cue for a behavior. For example, your dog comes to you when you say *Come,* but you would like to change the cue to *Here.* To make this change, use the new cue first *(Here),* pause, and then use the old cue *(Come).* As you continue this sequence, your dog will start to respond after the new cue and before the old one. You want to reinforce this response highly. Eventually, you will no longer need the old cue.

Remember, most dogs respond better to body language and hand signals than to verbal cues. If there is a discrepancy between what you say and what you do, your dog is most likely to respond to what you do regardless of what you say. For example, if you are running straight ahead with your dog toward a tunnel and tell him *Weave,* he is probably going to continue into the tunnel rather than looking around to find the weave poles. Many off-courses in agility result from handlers giving conflicting verbal cues and body language signals.

A dog fails to pick up on her handler's body language to turn right.

To start, your dog needs to be able to sit and remain sitting while you continually feed him small, soft treats (like feeding quarters into a slot machine). Feed in this manner for 30-second intervals, then release your dog from the sit and ignore him for 30 seconds. Repeat often. If your dog gets up during this process say Oops!, ask him to sit, and begin feeding again. Once your dog is sitting still for continual feeding, slow the rate of reinforcement to a treat every 3 to 5 seconds. Continue to gradually slow your rate of reinforcement until you are only feeding at the end of the 30-second interval. Next you should add distance, one step at a time, away from your dog. When you start adding distance, you will then need to return to a higher rate of reinforcement. This means that you will step away from your dog, step back to your dog, reinforce, then step away again. Continue in this fashion until your dog can stay for 30 seconds with you one step away before adding more distance. When your dog can stay for 30 seconds while you are six steps away, you can move on in your stay training.

Advanced stay training involves having someone else come in to feed your dog while you move even further away. This technique is very useful since your dog learns that staying in position, even when you are gone, will be reinforced. When your dog can hold his stay reliably in this situation, you can begin adding mild distractions. When you start adding distractions you should move back to your initial stages of continual feeding while you are next to your dog, then move forward as previously described as your dog becomes successful. Building your stay in small steps will lead to a strong, consistent behavior. Skipping steps and rushing ahead too quickly leads to stays that fall apart in competition. When your dog breaks a stay while training, the worst thing that ever happens is that you say Oops! and withhold the reinforcement. Our recommendation is that you release your dog from a stay using a verbal cue, given only while you are stationary. Releasing your dog while you are moving could confuse your dog.

A note on corrections for stays: At a recent agility trial, a long-time trainer of multiple OTCH (obedience trial champion) dogs told Deb with great certainty that, "You can't teach a fast dog a reliable stay on the start line." While Deb didn't say it, she thought, "Not if you use traditional obedience methods." Setting the dog up for failure so that you can go back and correct mistakes, as more traditional obedience competitors commonly do, will often lead to a stressed, nervous dog that is even less likely to stay in place, especially when highly aroused in agility. We find it interesting that many top agility trainers with extremely high-drive dogs have excellent start-line stays while some top obedience trainers have poor stays in the context of agility.

SELF-CONTROL

Besides responding to the trainer's direction, a dog also needs to learn to exhibit self-control. Rather than mindlessly responding to stimuli in the environment, a dog must inhibit his actions in certain situations. Below are several exercises that teach a dog the concept of self-control.

Impulse control: In this exercise the dog must learn to look to the handler for permission to take his reinforcer. Start this exercise with the dog on leash and toss a food treat on the ground in front of the dog. Make sure that you hold the leash so that the dog cannot reach the reinforcer. Simply wait until your dog finally looks back at you, use your behavioral marker, give a verbal release to get the treat, and move toward the treat with the dog if necessary. Repeat many times. At first it may take your dog some time to look at you and he may just give a quick glance in your general direction. That's okay; be ready to mark and release for that glance. You should notice that it will take less and less time for your dog to look away from the treat and back to you. In the more advanced stages of impulse control training, you will want to wait for more extended eye contact before marking and releasing to the treat. This exercise teaches the dog that the trainer is important and makes the decision about what he can and can't have. If your dog is highly toy motivated, you can practice this exercise with a favorite toy rather than a treat.

Doggie Zen: The basic purpose of this exercise is to teach the dog that giving up something he wants leads to getting what he wants. This is a variation of the impulse control exercise. After first showing a treat to the the dog, hold the treat in your closed fist and wait until the dog stops trying to get the treat and backs away slightly. Then mark and offer the treat. If the dog attempts to bite or scratch at your fist raise it up slightly until the dog settles, then put it back down again. Repeat until your dog backs away from your closed fist immediately.

***Slooooow* treats:** This self-control exercise teaches your dog that "good things come to those who wait." Use a low-value food reinforcer for this exercise. Ask your dog to sit, and then slowly begin to move a treat toward his mouth. If your dog moves toward the food, say *Oops!* and slowly move the treat away from your dog. When your dog is still, start moving the treat slowly toward his mouth again. You want your dog to learn that being still makes the treat come to him and moving toward it makes it go away. When you get the treat close to your dog's mouth while he is still, use your marker and let him have the treat. Once your

Smudge, Morgan, and Sabre exhibiting a high level of self-control.

dog seems to understand the exercise and can hold still while you slowly deliver the treat, you can move to higher-value food reinforcers.

Leave it: Another variation on the impulse control exercise is to teach your dog to move away from something he cannot have. We teach this command by having a helper hold something to entice the dog (low-value food or toy). When your dog is interested in the distraction, approach the dog, show him a high-value reinforcer, and lure him a few steps away. As the dog moves away from the helper, mark and treat. Allow the dog to approach the helper again, and lure him away with the high-value reinforcer. As you continue working on this exercise you should not have to move in as close to get your dog to come away from the distraction. Once your dog quickly moves away from the distraction, you can add the verbal cue *Leave it* immediately before you move in to lure the dog away. Make sure your *Leave it* cue is said in a happy voice, not a scolding tone.

Note: Working on control exercises may not be physically tiring, but for a high-drive dog these exercises can be mentally exhausting. They require intense concentration and self-control, which is difficult for certain dogs. Be careful not to overwhelm your dog with too many control exercises at one time. When practicing these exercises, be sure to only work for short periods. Take frequent breaks, turning your dog off, to give him a chance to relax.

Shifting Criteria

A *criterion* is the requirement or standard the trainer sets for a behavior. Three main criteria for a behavior are duration, distance, and distraction. When asking for more from your dog, it is critical to raise each criterion separately and in an organized fashion. That means that when you are starting to work on building duration of a behavior, you don't further confound the exercise with the challenge of greater distances and/or distractions. This practice will help your dog develop strong, precise, and accurate responses in all circumstances. In most situations you will want to raise the criteria for duration first, next distance, and then distraction. Whenever you add a new criterion, you will drop the requirements for the others to make it as easy as possible for your dog to be successful.

Duration is the length of time the dog must maintain the behavior. It is important to build duration slowly in the beginning, asking your dog to maintain the behavior only for a second at first and then increasing the duration by a second or two at a time. Trying to build duration too quickly will lead to too many errors, which frustrates both the dog and the trainer. When teaching your dog a sit- or a down-stay, for example, you would start by marking and rewarding a one-second stay with you standing at the dog's side. When your dog can hold a one-second stay, you would raise your duration criteria. In training duration, it is also important to vary the time requirement. Rather than always making it harder by asking for more, go back and reinforce shorter-duration stays as well. You might work on a stay by rewarding at two seconds, then four seconds, then six seconds, then two seconds again, always remaining at the dog's side. When starting to train duration, remember to lower any distance or distraction requirements.

Distance is the physical space between the trainer and the dog. In general, the greater the distance, the more difficult it is to get precise, reliable responses from the dog. You begin training distance by moving away slightly, possibly only a single step. Immediately use your behavioral marker and return to your dog to reward. Continue to move away from and then immediately back to your dog as long as he is being successful. Don't be afraid to back up to an easier level if your dog starts to make mistakes. As with duration, vary the distance requirements by rewarding some easier versions of the behavior along with more challenging ones. If you are working on a sit-stay, for example, you might reward at one step, three steps, five steps, and then two steps. When you start adding distance to an exercise or behavior you should drop the duration requirement as much as possible. Once you have achieved reliability at the desired distance, begin adding duration again.

A *distraction* is any stimulus that interferes with your dog's ability to maintain the required behavior. Distractions include other people and dogs, sounds, smells, strange situations, new places, and just about anything else that could claim your dog's attention. Deb's Golden Retriever Sully is highly distracted by shiny objects of any kind, including aluminum foil. Once at an obedience trial the judge was wearing a sparkly sweater studded with rhinestones. During the stand for exam exercise, Sully was so fascinated by the sweater that he nearly fell over while trying to watch the judge as she examined him.

Distraction should be the last criterion that you add to any behavior. Keeping distraction levels low at first gives your dog the best possible opportunity to concentrate and succeed. When your dog clearly can meet the duration and distance requirements for an exercise, you can introduce mild distractions. Determining whether a distraction is mild, moderate, or extreme is an individual judgment call. At first, introduce distractions to your dog at a low level. Increase the level of distractions slowly and carefully. Lower the duration and distance criteria when you start. It is also important to remember that changing the location in which you train may add enough distraction in itself. Sometimes simply moving to a different part of the room is enough of a change. In Deb's training classes, she has students practice in one place for a few minutes, then move to a different spot in the room and perform the same exercise. Surprisingly, dogs that could perform well in one place act as if they have no idea what to do once they move to another spot in the same room. Any new location can have a whole set of distracting elements, such as different sights, sounds, and smells.

©FREEZE FRAME FOTO

Use distractions to their full advantage: Look at them as training opportunities. Instead of trying to avoid them, seek them out and train through them. For example, Sabre was highly distracted by another dog (Quick, a Belgian Malinois) at Judy's training club. He fixated on her when she practiced, barking and attempting to chase her if possible. It was extremely difficult for him to focus on Judy when Quick was out on the training floor. At this point, it was time to pull out the high-value reinforcers. Judy also had to prevent Sabre from having the opportunity to chase Quick by keeping him on leash. We needed to prevent the unwanted behavior from happening so that we could get and reinforce a more acceptable response. In addition, we needed to move Sabre far enough away when Quick was working so that he could actually pay attention to Judy. Whenever Sabre glanced in Judy's direction, she clicked and treated. Instead of asking him to pay attention to her, she simply waited for him to offer attention, which she then reinforced highly. When Sabre was able to pay attention to Judy while Quick was working, they moved closer to the action. Again, Judy simply waited for Sabre to offer attention and was ready to capture and reward well for it. The next step was to ask for a sit while Quick was running. When Sabre could respond regularly, Judy started adding a duration requirement to the sit. Once Sabre could hold a solid sit-stay, Judy began putting distance between her and Sabre. After working slowly and carefully through those steps, Sabre now can hold a sit-stay at a distance from Judy while Quick works.

Some distractions are much more difficult to ignore than others

MOVING CONTROL

Before you add too much movement to your control work, be sure that your dog can perform the control exercises described above reliably. Adding movement to your training program greatly increases the difficulty of the exercises.

Controlled walking: Do not start this exercise until your dog is proficient at coming in to both sides. In controlled walking your dog should walk next to you on the desired side and at the same speed that you are moving. Your dog should speed up and slow down with you. Be sure that your dog stays parallel to you and does not race ahead. Start controlled walking with just a step or two, marking and treating your dog for moving with you. As your dog becomes successful, increase the number of steps you take before reinforcing. Once your dog can move with you at a normal pace, then you can add slow and fast changes of pace. If you have a dog that consistently wants to move ahead of you, it is a good idea

to mark and then toss the reinforcer *behind* the dog to keep him from focusing forward as much. We use this technique often with Sabre. If you have a Velcro dog (a dog that wants to stay glued to your side and not move ahead), it is a good idea to mark and then toss the reinforcer *ahead* of the dog to encourage him to move forward confidently. We use this technique often with Copper.

Let's go: Once you have mastered controlled walking, you can take this exercise to the next level by adding running to it. Use an exciting verbal prompt as you encourage your dog to run along with you. Keep connected to your dog by using praise. Your dog does not need to maintain strict eye contact but must be responsive to you. Run and then slow down in short, intense spurts. You want your dog to run parallel to you at approximately the same speed. If your dog tends to forge ahead of you, turn away from him and run in the opposite direction, encouraging him to catch up. Be sure to reinforce your dog for catching you. Practice this exercise with your dog on both your left and right sides.

CROSSES

The purpose of a cross is to change the side of your body that your dog is working on. The types of turns and crosses you may use on an agility course depend on the nature of the course, your dog, and your physical abilities. Most people find it useful to be able to perform at least some of these maneuvers. We will give a brief general description of each move, but it is best to get in-person instruction from a knowledgeable agility trainer.

Front cross: You will use the front cross as a way to switch sides when you are ahead of your dog. You will turn toward your dog, cueing your dog to turn toward you so he ends up on the opposite side of your body. Kathy Keats explains teaching the front cross in "Agility Basics for Canines and Competitors," *Clean Run*, May and June 2003 (CR Vol. 9, #5 and #6.)

Rear cross: You will use the rear cross as a way to switch sides when you are behind your dog. As the dog moves ahead, you will cross behind, which will cue your dog to turn in the new direction, and continue with your dog on the opposite side. See "Agility Basics for Canines and Competitors," *Clean Run*, February 2003 (Vol. 9, #2) for extensive steps in teaching the flip, turning the dog away from you, an essential element of the rear cross.

Blind cross: As with the front cross, the blind cross is used to switch sides when you are ahead of your dog. Instead of turning into your dog, you will continue moving forward ahead of your dog and cross his path, so he ends up on your opposite side.

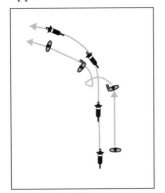

Front cross: handler crosses in front of dog

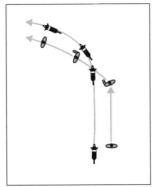

Rear cross: handler crosses behind dog

Blind cross: handler crosses in front of dog

AGILITY HEELING

Once you have mastered the basic moving control exercises, you can put them all together to practice agility heeling. Agility heeling gives you the opportunity to perform all the basic agility moves without equipment. It is also an excellent way to improve your teamwork and your dog's responsiveness to your cues. We recommend that you use a combination of verbal cues, body language, and hand signals during agility heeling. Start out slowly at first and only try one or two moves at a time. It will take you a while to feel comfortable going through the agility moves at a normal and at a fast pace with your dog. If you feel unsure about performing this exercise, check with your agility instructor for feedback and suggestions.

Varying the Reinforcement Schedule

The goal of most training is to move to a thin schedule of reinforcement. This means that the dog consistently performs the desired behavior but only occasionally receives a marker and reward. When teaching new behaviors, dogs need to receive continuous reinforcement. You need to mark and reinforce every correct behavior (or attempt at a correct behavior). Besides rewarding desired behavior, marking and reinforcing also provide the dog information that he is doing, or attempting to do, the right thing.

Once a behavior has been learned, however, it will be maintained much more strongly on a variable, rather than continuous, schedule of reinforcement. You can start moving to variable reinforcement once the dog performs the behavior reliably when you give the cue. Two types of variable reinforcement that are useful in dog training are variable ratio (the number of times a behavior is performed) and variable duration (the amount of time a dog must maintain a behavior).

Most people begin variable ratio training by moving to reinforcing after two or three correct behaviors. As long as the dog continues to respond properly, you can move to reinforcing after four or five correct behaviors on occasion, then move back to fewer. To be truly variable, the reinforcement must occur randomly, with no set pattern. To be effective, it is best to raise and lower the number of required behaviors so that you can reinforce the dog on a regular basis. You are more likely to keep the dog engaged and working if you mark and reward according to a random pattern, such as after the following numbers of sits: 2, 1, 3, 1, 2, 4, 1. If you set your requirements too high, your dog may give up when he doesn't get reinforced fairly quickly.

In variable duration training, reinforcement should occur at random times. Marking and rewarding a down-stay after two seconds, then three seconds, then five seconds, then one second, then four seconds, then two seconds, allows the dog to be successful and should help maintain his interest. The time requirements can be increased as the dog seems ready, but you should always throw in some quick reinforcements as a way to keep your dog engaged and successful.

Front cross on the flat   *Rear cross on the flat*   *Let's go*

Agility heeling can include controlled walking, *Let's go*, and front, rear, and blind crosses. Be surprising and exciting during this exercise. Keep each sequence of agility heeling relatively short (no more than 1 to 2 minutes) and reinforce your dog multiple times *during* each sequence. You can mark and treat for attention, a quick response, a nice cross, and so on, then simply continue with the sequence. Release your dog for a minute or so between each sequence and allow him to relax. Remember to practice all your moving exercises with your dog on both your left and right sides.

Some examples of agility heeling would be:

- Start with a quick *Let's go*, take a few steps, do a front cross, slow down into controlled walking for a few steps, and then do a blind cross.
- Start with slow controlled walking, suddenly increase to a fast pace, do a rear cross, change back to a slow pace, do a front cross, increase to a moderate pace for a few steps, and do a blind cross.
- From a stationary position do a front cross, then move into a fast pace for a few steps, go into a slow pace, then do a blind cross.

Try lots of combinations and variations. You are only limited by your imagination.

As we mentioned before, it is *extremely* important to reinforce your dog multiple times during the agility heeling sequences. The purpose of this exercise is to practice and perfect the small movements that lead to success in the agility ring. To get this kind of responsiveness and precision, you need to capture those moments and reinforce them.

In example #1 above, there are many opportunities to reinforce specific behaviors. You could mark and treat when your dog moves into a fast pace with you, mark and treat again after the front cross, mark and treat again when your dog slows into controlled walking, and then mark and treat the blind cross.

Developing a Working Relationship with Your Performance Dog

ADVANCED AGILITY HEELING

Once your dog can successfully perform agility heeling then you can add some advanced variations to increase the difficulty. Some examples would include:

Treat toss: When you are giving your dog his treat for a good performance in advanced agility heeling, toss the treat behind him for him to turn and chase. When he gets to his treat, you will start moving forward. Your dog should soon realize that you are heeling without him and catch up with you. You can call his name and encourage him to come toward you. Be sure to mark and reward when he reaches your side. If your dog runs past you rather than moving to your side, turn quickly and move in the opposite direction. His job is to find his position at your side. If your dog does not try to move toward you, move faster so that you are more exciting and interesting.

Run away: In this variation of the treat toss, you toss your dog's treat behind him, then run away from him. This should encourage your dog to quickly get his treat then race to catch up with you. Don't slow down and wait for your dog; keep moving quickly until your dog gets to you. Mark and reward when he reaches your side.

Silent agility heeling: To help your dog focus on your body language and movement rather than your voice, you can practice agility heeling without any verbal cues or prompts. Your dog's job is to pay close attention to you to catch your movements and signals. Be sure to reinforce often when beginning this exercise to let your dog know that he is doing the right thing.

Stays: To increase your control over your dog's movement, you can add sit-, down-, and stand-stays to your agility heeling exercises. When your dog is moving well at your side stop and ask him to sit. Tell him to stay, and then walk away. Mark and toss him his treat. When you can walk away easily, you can move further away before you reward. When he can manage the further distance easily, you can move away at a faster pace. Later you might circle him at a walk before rewarding. About three-quarters of the time, reward him while he's in the stay. About one-quarter of the time, call him from the stay to your side. For the down-stay you may need to pivot in front of your dog to stop his forward motion, then ask for a down. The stand-stay is often the most difficult position for dogs to hold. Don't try to move away too far or too quickly. Reinforce while your dog is being successful and you are still close. Follow the same guidelines for the stand- and down-stays of rewarding the dog in the stay three-quarters of the time and calling him to your side one-quarter of the time.

The ultimate goal of moving control training is to develop the precision and responsiveness of your dog to your body language, hand signals, and verbal cues, here exemplified by Stacy Peardot-Goudy and her border collie Secret.

Circles and turns: These include turns of 180° and circles of 360°. In a 180° turn (about turn) the dog and handler turn together and end up heading in the opposite direction. During the turn the dog should maintain his position at your side. In a 360° turn the dog and handler move together in a full circle and end up heading in the same direction with the dog on the same side as he started. Both of these moves can be performed with the dog on either the inside or the outside path.

Equipment: One of the final steps in training agility heeling is to practice around and between agility obstacles. Start by adding your dog's least favorite pieces of equipment before putting out the ones that are a bigger temptation to your dog. At first, practice with only a few pieces of equipment and keep some distance from it as you work. Gradually decrease that distance and then add more equipment as your dog becomes more able to focus on you and ignore the distractions. In the final stages of agility heeling, you may add the performance of a piece of equipment as part of your training. For example, if your dog likes the tunnel, you can work on controlled walking around the tunnel and release him to perform the tunnel as his reward.

Boosting Speed

The term *latency* refers to the period between giving the cue for a behavior and its occurrence. In the fast-paced sport of agility, a short latency is vital. If the dog responds, but does so too slowly, he may miss the obstacle or turn that was indicated by the handler. Or the dog may follow all the handler's directions and cues but do so at a slow enough pace to earn time faults. The antidote therefore is: always strive for rapid-fire responses from your dog in training. Many trainers say that you should train as if you were trialing.

A dog may respond slowly due to confusion, a lack of training, low motivation, or because the desired behavior is physically difficult (which makes a faster response impossible). The physical aspect may be the result of structural problems or minor injuries due to the demands of the sport. Trainers should address and resolve these possibilities before considering training solutions.

A dog may respond slowly because he is uncertain about how to perform the behavior. For example, we have seen dogs that race up the A-frame, slow down at the top, and creep down slat by slat. Many times, these dogs (and their trainers) are uncertain about the desired contact-zone performance, so they slow down to avoid a mistake.

A slow obstacle performance also may be due to incorrect initial training. Some dogs learned to weave and can complete the weaves correctly but cross over their front feet between each weave, leading to a time-consuming performance. Trying to speed up this behavior would lead to stumbling and skipping poles. Instead, it is necessary to retrain weave footwork to significantly speed up weave pole performance. (See photographs, opposite page.)

A dog may perform slowly due to stress and worry. The trainer needs to address the cause of the fear and concern so that the dog is more relaxed and comfortable while doing agility. See "Stress Kills Fun" (page 60) for ideas on dealing with these problems.

Sometimes a dog starts trialing with lots of speed and then slows down as he moves into the upper levels of competition. Certainly increased course difficulty can slow a dog. Also, as the course requirements become more difficult, the handler may become more stressed and nervous and transmit these emotions to the dog. The dog then comes to feel that there is something worrisome about performing agility. The dog slows down, causing the handler even

©WENDY BEARD

©CINDY TELLEY

©ARDIS LUKENS

Taking the time to train this lab's weaving footwork paid off big time in boosting her drive and speed through the poles.

more stress, which when transmitted to the dog, slows him down even further in a vicious cycle. The way out of this trap is to build confidence through positive, consistent training. Removing the stress of showing while working on fun and exciting training games, and setting the dog up for success rather than failure will help make agility a more enjoyable experience for both dog and trainer.

It is also possible that a dog has learned to perform an obstacle or behavior properly but has been rewarded for a slow but correct performance. To increase his speed, the trainer could use a *limited hold* technique. A limited hold means that, once the handler has given the cue, the clock starts ticking, and the dog has a specific time frame in which to complete the behavior to earn rewards. If he is too slow, the trainer withholds any really good rewards. Before using this technique, you need to establish a baseline average performance time. Have the dog perform the obstacle or behavior four to five times while someone with a stopwatch times your dog. Then compute the average. While training, mark and reward only those performances that are under the baseline time. Over time, you will find speed increasing. Then you can compute a new, lower average baseline and only reinforce performances below that time. If your dog performs correctly, but over baseline time, then you can give him praise and a pat, but no food, toy, or play reinforcers. The really good stuff only happens when your dog meets the time limit.

If your dog cannot beat baseline time, or he gets slower rather than faster, you need to make some adjustments. You may need to make the behavior easier and work on incorporating more motivation (higher value reinforcers and more play and games) into the exercise. Or, you may need to raise the baseline by a few seconds and then lower it as your dog becomes successful.

ORGANIZED CONTROL

To increase your control over your dog's behavior you need to work on the following aspects of the FOCUS program:

1. Control all the resources in your dog's environment. Everything needs to come through you.

2. Introduce and train the stationary control exercises in a systematic manner.

3. Add difficulty to the stationary exercises, being sure that you build up your dog's confidence and success through reinforcement.

4. Practice the self-control exercises with your dog, adding difficulty to each exercise as he is successful.

5. Add the moving control exercises when your dog finds the stationary and self-control exercises fairly easy.

6. Strive for ultimate control by adding verbal cues and signals, shifting criteria, and moving to variable reinforcement.

Step Three: Consistency

Sabre's Story: *Maintain what you gain*

Once Sabre discovered that following Judy's direction was necessary for the fun to continue, his agility performances improved dramatically. But we weren't finished training at that point. If Judy had not been consistent in her expectations, it would have been easy for Sabre to regress to earlier, "bad" habits once he went back into the ring. It was critical for Judy to maintain her criteria for acceptable performance both in training and in trialing. The fun had to end immediately if Sabre was not paying attention to Judy. On the other hand, if Sabre did listen and respond correctly, not only did he get to continue playing agility, but he also got extra reinforcers (jackpot, playing ball, taking a long walk, and so on) at the end of his run. Sabre quickly learned that it was in his best interest to cooperate.

FOLLOW THROUGH

How can you keep the progress you've made? If you've been working consistently with the FOCUS program, you've done your homework. The good news is you're well on your way, but you're not done training. To keep the progress you've made, you need to move to the maintenance phase of the program. It will be easy for your dog to regress to old, undesired behavior patterns (not having enough fun or having too much fun) if you don't carefully monitor and control training and trialing experiences.

Letting little problems and mistakes slide will lead to bigger problems and mistakes. It is vital to maintain your training criteria in *all* situations. This is the trainer's responsibility, not the dog's. Left to his own devices, your dog likely will regress. If you want to make the new behavior patterns solid and permanent, you will need to be dedicated to maintenance. Consistency in your expectations will lead to consistent responses from the dog. Those responses will be the foundation for new behavior patterns.

A big part of maintaining new responses is teaching your dog that certain relationships between events are always true. For example, a click is always followed by a reinforcer. That relationship is a contingency. One thing always leads to the other. A contingency makes events orderly and predictable. When you put your key in the ignition and turn it, your car usually starts. That's also a contingency. When the phone rings and you answer it, there's usually someone on the line. That's a contingency, too. We have learned that one event (turning the key in the ignition; answering a ringing phone) usually leads to an expected result (the car starts; someone is on the line). If, occasionally, the car doesn't start or there's no one on the phone line, we might dismiss that as an unusual event. The more often those "unusual events" happen, however, the less certain we become about whether the contingency actually exists. If people, with our supposedly superior powers of reasoning, can become confused, imagine how your dog feels when you are inconsistent in your expectations.

Dogs are good at learning contingencies. They can learn that behaving in certain ways leads to predictable consequences. It is your job as a trainer to keep the contingencies in place. You need to be clear about what you find to be acceptable and unacceptable behaviors, and have a clear plan for providing consequences for each.

TRIALING ISSUES

In the August 2003 issue of *Clean Run* magazine Kathy Keats wrote an editorial titled "But it Only Happens at Trials." In that editorial she discussed the importance of a testing phase to determine your dog's level of progress and need for further training. In the testing phase, you enter your dog in a trial or two, note any areas that need further work, and then go back to training for a while before testing your dog again. Unfortunately, many trainers move from training to competing, whether or not their dogs might benefit from more intensive training without the added pressure of trial performance. Continuing to compete in trials when the dog is not solid on obstacle performances, or when the dog needs more confidence or more control work, can be damaging to the dog's future agility career. We are *not* saying that the dog needs to be perfect to compete. We *are* saying that the trainer should be using trials (especially early in the dog's career or after a break to work on FOCUS) as diagnostic tools to guide further training.

It is important to carefully consider your dog's first trials. These initial experiences may strongly determine your dog's general attitude toward agility trials. For many dogs it might be a good idea to choose smaller, indoor trials without much commotion and distraction. Making your dog's first trials as relaxed and enjoyable as possible will pay big dividends. Most handlers, even experienced ones, are excited and nervous when showing a young dog for the first time, but good handlers will concentrate on making sure the dog is comfortable in the show setting and having a good ring experience. At this point, being concerned with perfect performances and qualifying scores should be secondary to helping the dog develop a positive emotional response to showing.

Making sure that your dog has good initial ring experiences doesn't mean that "anything goes" in the ring. It means that you will make the effort to help your dog get it right, even if that means slowing down, giving some extra encouragement, and giving liberal praise for correct performance. If your dog makes mistakes in the ring, those mistakes should give you information about what you need to work on in training. If your dog makes a mistake in the ring once, it is unlikely to become a habit if you stop showing while you work on training a more solid behavior. If your dog makes the same mistake repeatedly and you continue showing, however, you are setting yourself up for long-term problems. For example, allowing your dog to break his start-line stay and continuing to run the course teaches him that the rules differ between training and showing. The same confusion arises if your dog has been trained for a two-on/two-off contact performance, but you let him jump off and continue running at a trial. In both examples, you are being inconsistent in your expectations and confusing your dog about the required performance at a show.

You should have a primary goal for each ring experience. For example, in Deb's first trial with Luna, her only goal was to keep Luna focused on her rather than on all the distractions in the environment. When Judy put Sabre back into the ring after four months of working on the FOCUS program, her goal was to complete the course with Sabre under control and listening to direction. In both of these cases, qualifying scores would have been a nice plus, but they were not the main objective.

We recently observed handlers at a USDAA trial playing Snooker. The A-frame was worth 7 points and many handlers went for the top score, attempting three 7s. Many also allowed their dogs to jump off the A-frame without even touching the contact each time, even though they were requiring two-on/two-off contact performances in training. This clear inconsistency between training and trialing is guaranteed to set back their contact training, especially if contact performance is an ongoing problem, or the dog is in the early stages of his show career .

Once people have started showing in agility and enjoying the trial experience (the rush of adrenaline during a run is definitely addictive), it is difficult to stop and go back to training. Continuing to show while trying to change certain behaviors, however, can confuse the dog and also frustrate and become expensive for the handler. Taking a time out for more training often is the best way to correct problems before they become too ingrained. If your dog's overall performance is beginning to suffer (your dog is getting slower and slower and becoming increasingly distracted or out of control), you need to get out of the ring and work on FOCUS.

TRAINING/TRIALING DISTINCTION

How many times have you heard someone say, "But it only happens in trials!" According to these trainers, the dog is perfect in training, never breaks a stay, never misses a contact, always performs weaves perfectly, and so on. So what causes the difference in your dog's performance between training and trialing? A strong possibility may be that your training sessions do not provide the same levels of excitement, distraction, and pressure (for both you and your dog) as a trial does. As the trainer, it is your job to plan training sessions that are appropriate for your dog's level of progress but that are also challenging enough to improve your dog's performance. It is easy to go through the motions in training without addressing your dog's problem areas. One of the main differences between training and trialing are the levels of stress, arousal, and excitement for both handler and dog, but there are ways to bring that high level of excitement and arousal into your training sessions. It takes some creative thinking and planning, but it is definitely worth the effort.

Demand in the ring what you expect in training.

Sabre's Story: Sabre versus the vacuum

When you have a highly driven dog, sometimes you have to go to great lengths to teach a reliable stay. Sabre's vacuum story shows how we found a way to make training as exciting and challenging as trialing. Outside of agility, the most exciting event in Sabre's life is the appearance of the vacuum cleaner. Simply saying the word

"vacuum" sent him into a frenzy of leaping, spinning, and barking. Since this response most closely approximated Sabre's level of excitement in the agility ring, we decided to use the vacuum in training him to stay. If he could stay while the vacuum was running, he could stay through anything. In the beginning, Sabre could barely hold a sit while Judy walked to the closet door where the vacuum lives. With Deb continually feeding Sabre, she worked through walking to the closet, opening the closet door, taking out the vacuum, rolling it into the room, plugging it in, turning it on, and running it. Each action required going back to step one in stay training, then moving forward from there. It took quite a bit of practice before Sabre could hold a solid stay in the face of this huge distraction, but the ability to overcome this distraction carried over into the agility ring. Sabre's vacuum training produced very solid start-line and table stays.

Perhaps your dog has learned that training and trialing are two very different events with different expectations, requirements, and consequences. Think about all the aspects that are different between the two situations. In training the handler experiences much less stress. If you make a mistake, you can go back and fix it. A run doesn't cost $20 and there's no qualifying score to worry about. Since the handler's stress level is usually directly transmitted to the dog, this difference alone is enough to change the dog's ring performance. For the dog that already isn't having enough fun in agility, the increased stress level is likely to make him even slower and more distracted. In contrast, the dog that already is having too much fun is likely to get overexcited and aroused due to the handler's stress level and to act even more out of control than usual.

One way to raise the excitement and stress level in a class setting is to use a racing game. Having two dogs and handlers compete over identical short sequences (often jump, weaves, jump, tunnel, and back) is guaranteed to put both pairs of handlers and dogs into an emotional state that more accurately resembles show conditions. You can replace the weaves with a piece of contact equipment for those who have contact problems in trials, but not in training. Relay races with teams will raise stress and excitement levels as well. These types of games are good tests to see how ready teams are to withstand the emotional pressure of competition.

REGRESSION

Sabre's Story: Oh no! Back to the beginning?

After four months out of the ring and working consistently on FOCUS, Sabre went back into trialing. We had a plan for dealing with mistakes due to lack of control (Sabre's big problem). Judy kept a tight rein on Sabre in the ring, calling him close to her side to keep him focused on her, and placing him in a down to settle him if he went over the top. Sabre's ring performances improved dramatically. For five months of trialing, he continued getting better and better. Then, Sabre made a mistake in the ring and Judy let it slide. He came blasting out of the chute and cut behind her, leaping, spinning, and barking. Rather than stopping the fun immediately (the usual contingency), Judy regrouped and continued running. That, unfortunately, was a big mistake. That same weekend Sabre slid slightly on the flooring and missed his weave entry. Again, Judy let the error go and continued, reasoning that he couldn't be held responsible for the footing. While that is true, for Sabre it was another big mistake. Sabre needed it to be crystal clear that the consequence for failing to perform an obstacle on the first try was leaving the ring. From that point on, the "old Sabre" was back—the one that went into run mode and didn't listen to direction.

To regress means to move backward. Unfortunately for trainers, regression happens. Even if you've worked and worked to change your dog's behavior, and "done everything right," your dog may still regress, reverting to older, less desirable behaviors. Retrained behaviors are never as strong as the original ones and will always require more maintenance. Under pressure, dogs often revert to the first thing they learned (called a *default behavior*). After working hard to retrain undesirable behaviors, it is important to closely monitor those behaviors for signs of regression and to respond to those signs by continually reinforcing the new behaviors at a high level.

For the trainer it can be devastating to see the results of months of work seemingly vanish in an instant. Behaviorists know, however, that instances of regression, often called *spontaneous recovery*, are highly likely to occur. The term spontaneous recovery actually refers to recovering the older, initial response. This trend is normal, even if it is undesirable. Behaviorists also know that they can work through spontaneous recovery and that it will typically disappear if the new contingencies remain consistent. The tendency for those unaware of the possibility of working through regression is either to give up at this point or to try something completely different. Neither of these courses of action is going to help. Instead, move your training back a few steps to help your dog be successful. Don't change your overall requirements and expectations, but do lower them in training for a short time until the dog starts responding correctly, then raise them again.

In considering whether to be concerned about undesired responses and behaviors, obedience trainers go by the rule: "Once is a fluke, twice is a trend, three times is a lifestyle." A single error or mistake is not necessarily cause for panic. There are several reasons why a mistake might occur once in any given setting. Just as people, dogs sometimes make mistakes for no particular reason. In an obedience trial, Deb once attempted to call her young dog but mistakenly used her older dog's name. Clearly, she knew the correct behavior (calling the dog's name), but a momentary lapse in concentration caused an error. Handlers make mistakes in the ring all the time yet don't become overly concerned about any individual error unless they see a clear pattern. Mistakes can happen because of a moment's inattention, a high-level distraction, or undue stress.

If you see the same or a similar error happen more than once, however, take that as a warning sign. The emerging pattern should tell you that it's definitely time to do something about the problem behavior in training. If your training efforts don't have the desired effect on the performance in trials, then it's definitely time to get out of the ring until you can retrain more intensively. Allowing the dog to continue making the same mistake over and over in trials simply reinforces the undesired behavior.

SO, HOW DO I FIX THIS?

Sabre's Story: No quick fixes

Both Deb and Judy were taken aback by Sabre's regression. Judy was disheartened over the months and months of intensive retraining that seemed to lead her right back to where she had started. Though Deb knew that regression was a strong possibility, it was still an unpleasant fact to face. What Deb also knew, though,  *was that this was the time to be consistent, keep those contingencies in place, and continue working on strengthening the desired behaviors in training. Sabre went through a phase where he tested every behavior they had retrained, and he found that the same consequences would always be true whether in training, runthroughs, or trials. Following direction and maintaining self-control led to a food jackpot, praise, playing ball, sitting with Judy ringside, and all kinds of fun stuff. Ignoring direction and losing control led to a quick quiet trip to the car or crate. Gradually, the new desirable behaviors reappeared.*

There is no magic pill to fix behavior and training problems. There is also no simple formula or plan to apply. You need to know your dog well and to have a good grasp of the consequences that are important for your dog. For dogs that love agility, leaving the ring suddenly may be an effective negative consequence. For this consequence to be effective and clear to the dog, however, the handler's timing must be ideal. You must take your dog from the ring as soon as the undesired behavior occurs. If the dog takes another obstacle after the mistake, the reason for leaving the ring will be confusing. For some dogs, leaving the ring may be a positive consequence. If a dog is stressed or uncertain, lacks confidence, or is not having enough fun, leaving the ring may be a relief. This is why it is so important to understand your dog. Applying an inappropriate consequence may have a devastating effect.

Some trainers ignore performance problems and training problems and assume that as the dog matures these problems will disappear. Allowing undesirable behaviors to continue in the hopes that they will magically vanish when the dog reaches a certain age is wishful thinking. Maturity alone does not solve training problems. All you will have is an older dog well practiced in incorrect behaviors. "Practice *does* makes perfect," whether the behavior is desirable or undesirable. It is reasonable, however, to expect a younger dog with less performance experience to be a little more excitable and less steady. It is not reasonable to use immaturity as an excuse for lack of training and inconsistent expectations.

When a dog performs an unexpected and undesirable behavior in the ring, the handler often panics. Rather than taking an error as feedback on problems to address in training, some handlers rush to fix the problem rather than going back to foundation work. The problem with quick fixes is that they are often short-term solutions for long-term problems. They may work quickly, but the effects usually disappear just as quickly.

Often handlers will ask (and receive) advice from others on ways to change their dogs' performances. Most dog trainers are happy to share their advice and opinions with others, but it's important to take that advice selectively. While advice may be given with good intentions, another trainer's solutions may not be the best choice for your dog. It's always good to listen to other people's opinions, but be careful what you apply to your training. Jumping from one training technique to another looking for the perfect solution may simply end up frustrating you and confusing your dog. Again, it's a case of knowing your dog well and incorporating new training ideas and techniques based on that knowledge.

You can't fix a behavior that doesn't already occur regularly. Something that occurs infrequently and inconsistently has never really been learned. You need to go back to square one and train it correctly. At a seminar a handler asked us to help her work on her dogwalk contact, saying that it was fine in training, but the dog leaped over the contact in the ring. What we saw was that the dog only performed the contact consistently when the handler was ahead of the dog, pointing at the contact, and saying *Right here*. When we asked her to hang back behind the dog (her normal position in the ring due to her dog's speed), the dog had no idea what to do at the end of the dogwalk. This is a case of the dog not truly understanding the requirements of the behavior. This problem cannot be fixed without going back and training the expected behavior from the beginning.

If you can't get the desired behavior in training, your odds of getting it in the ring are slim.

When considering ways to deal with training and performance problems, always go back to basics first. In training, lower your requirements and expectations so that your dog can be successful. Make the desired behaviors stronger by using high-value reinforcers. One of Sabre's major problems was running past the dogwalk rather than performing it. When Sabre regressed, he started running past the dogwalk again. In training, we made the dogwalk easier both by lowering it and by lowering our expectations to having him simply put a foot on the up ramp to earn reinforcement. We also used his highest value reinforcer (baby food) for this exercise. Going back to this earlier stage in training helped Sabre be successful. We then increased our requirements for reinforcement slowly and systematically, moving to reinforcing for two feet on the up ramp, then three, then all four, then for actually ascending the ramp. When he was performing the dogwalk at the lower height, we raised it slightly and began reinforcing for one foot, two feet, and so on, on the ramp again.

RITUALS

A ritual involves always performing the same series of behaviors in the same way in a specific situation. Many performers and athletes follow specific rituals before events. A useful ritual provides both mental and physical preparation for an upcoming activity. Rituals can provide a sense of familiarity and consistency in high stress situations. Developing and regularly performing warm-up rituals can help agility dogs and their handlers prepare mentally and physically for competition.

There are many activities and behaviors that can become part of a warm-up ritual. The exact nature of an effective ritual will depend, in large part, on your dog's agility personality. Dogs that are not having enough fun need to be energized and excited before running. They may need more physically engaging activities. On the other hand, dogs that are having too much fun may need to be kept physically calmer and quieter, and engaged in more mental activities.

For instance, when Deb is getting Copper ready to run she wants to get him very excited and encourages him to do physical tricks like stretching, spinning, running backward, and jumping up. She plays the Two Treats game to get him running back and forth and tolerates his enthusiastic barking. Copper's warm-up ritual is designed to get him highly active, motivated, and ready to run. To perform at his best, he needs to feel confident and full of himself.

When Judy is getting Sabre ready to run, she wants him to be very calm, cool, and collected. Her warm-up focuses on the control exercises such as controlled walking, calling him *Close* and *Side* from a distance, and practicing turns, sits, and downs. She also reinforces him highly when he offers her attention rather than focusing on the environment. Sabre's warm-up ritual is designed to keep him engaged with Judy and to keep his excitement level low. To perform at his best, he needs to be calm and in control of himself.

Regular, predictable rituals at the start line help your dog focus and feel more confident about the job at hand.

Another place where a ritual can be useful is setting up on the start line before a run. Following the same series of steps before running cues your dog about what's coming up next and helps your dog prepare. Whether you ask your dog for a sit, down, or stand before you begin, or take a running start with your dog is up to you. In general, dogs that aren't having enough fun do better with running starts, or a short wait at the start line. Dogs that are having too much fun may need to be trained in a more solid stay before being released to run. Asking for a long stay on the start line can be a problem for an unfocused, distracted dog. It would be much better to stay physically closer and remain mentally connected to this type of dog. You will have to experiment to find what works best for your dog. Whatever ritual you decide to use, use it regularly and predictably.

We recently observed a handler step up to the start line with her dog, put him in a sit stay, then watch the dog before her finish his run. Her dog paid close attention to her, but she paid no attention to him. Eventually, her dog gave up and looked away, at which point she turned her attention to him, noticed he was looking away, and commanded him to *Watch!* This mental disconnection between dog and handler just before a run can lead to problems on the course. It is critical that the handler is committed to maintaining FOCUS on the dog during warm-up and on the start line. As we have said before, FOCUS requires commitment from both dog and trainer; it is not one-sided. If you expect your dog's complete attention, then you should give your complete attention to your dog as well.

ORGANIZED CONSISTENCY

To remain consistent in your requirements and expectations, which in turn will maintain your dog's behavior and performance at the desired level, you should concentrate on the following aspects of the FOCUS program.

1. Follow through by maintaining your training criteria and contingencies. Be consistent by providing clear and fair consequences for behaviors.

2. As much as possible, train and trial in the same emotional state.

3. Use initial agility trials (in the beginning of your dog's career, or after time off to work on FOCUS) as a way to test the results of your training and to highlight areas for further work.

4. Be aware that changes in behavior and performance will not be quick and easy. They will require constant monitoring and generous reinforcement to maintain the desired behavior.

5. Expect regression as a natural part of the learning process. Maintain your criteria and work through setbacks.

6. Avoid the lure of quick fixes and taking free advice. Remember, there are no quick fixes, and you usually get what you pay for.

7. Develop and maintain performance rituals that prepare both you and your dog for training and competition.

Conclusion

Sabre's Story: The results

After showing for more than a year without earning an Excellent Standard leg, Sabre completed his AX title. We had been consistently working the FOCUS program with him for eight months. The last four months of the program he was actively showing and was listening well. His non-qualifying runs were due to handling and  *communication problems, not to lack of attention and focus. In fact, the change in Sabre's ring behavior was the cause of these problems. Judy had to learn how to handle the new Sabre—the one that was paying attention and trying to work with her. After working through the regression phase for several months, Sabre came back (in two trial weekends) to earn his first three MX legs, his first Double Q, finish his MXJ, and place third in a competitive International class.*

Your level of success using the FOCUS program depends on your commitment and determination. Developing and nurturing FOCUS takes a significant amount of time and energy. It requires you to examine your interactions with your dog very carefully and to manage your dog's environment quite closely.

The FOCUS program is never finished. Think of it as a training lifestyle. Every moment with your dog is a training opportunity. Many are wasted and many are spent teaching (even unintentionally) the wrong thing. Learning to see and effectively use every training opportunity is one of the best things you can take away from this program.

Building a training relationship with your dog is different from simply existing with your dog in the same household. It is even different from training your dog. The training relationship is more complicated than teaching behaviors. It involves a much deeper connection, commitment, and mutual awareness for both dog and trainer. When you see dog and handler teams that perform as one, almost reading each other's minds, you are usually observing the results of the hard work and dedication required to build a strong training relationship. It isn't easy, but it is definitely worth the time and effort.

Further Resources

AGILITY

Clean Run is the premier online source for books and videos on agility, training, and performance issues. You can browse the store at www.cleanrun.com.

Magazines:

Clean Run magazine focuses on agility but also presents useful information on positive training methods. For more information, click on www.cleanrun.com.

Internet Resources:

The **AGILEDOGS** list (www.cleanrun.com/agilelist.cfm) discusses agility-related training techniques, trial results and brags, questions and answers about rules, and so on.

Agility Ability (www.agilityability.com) provides general information about agility and links to other agility information on the web. People new to the sport should find the "Jump Into Agility" section particularly useful.

Clean Run (groups.yahoo.com/group/CleanRun) is a list for discussing dog agility training, handling sequences, and articles in Clean Run magazine.

Dog Agility Page (www.dogpatch.org/agility) lists just about everything related to agility on the web.

OPERANT CONDITIONING AND CLICKER TRAINING

Clean Run carries a wide variety of books on operant conditioning and clicker training as well as clicker training supplies. For more information, click on www.cleanrun.com.

Dogwise (formerly Direct Book Service) is an excellent mail order source for books and videos on clicker training and operant conditioning. You can request a catalog by calling (800) 776-2665 or ordering online at www.dogwise.com.

4-M Enterprises is another mail order source that carries clicker-related books and videos. They can be reached at (510) 489-8722.

Books:

Clicker Fun: Teaching Tricks and Games Using Positive Reinforcement. Deborah Jones, Ph.D. (1998). An introduction to clicker training presenting enjoyable ways to teach tricks and games.

Culture Clash: A Revolutionary New Way of Understanding the Relationship Between Humans and Domestic Dogs. Jean Donaldson. (1996). Excellent! Provides solid operant conditioning principles and highlights the philosophy that underlies approaches to dog training.

A Dog and a Dolphin 2.0. Karen Pryor. (1996). A great booklet to help new clicker trainers get started.

Videos:

Clicker Fun series. Deborah Jones, Ph.D. (1999). 30 minutes each. Contains footage for learning the basic clicker training skill that is useful for both beginner and more advanced clicker trainers. *Click & Go* is the basic getting-started resource that presents common terminology and techniques. *Click & Fix* shows positive ways to solve behavior problems.

Sniffy the Virtual Rat. Available as a CD-ROM with a manual through Thomson Publishing's website, Sniffy is a video game to help students learn all aspects of operant and classical conditioning using a hands-on approach. The less technical 'lite' version shows how learning theories apply to animal behavior.

Internet Resources:

There are masses of information about clicker training on the internet. Check out some of these sites, or simply type "clicker training" into any search engine.

www.clickersolutions.com
www.karenpryor.com
www.hsnp.com
www.inch.com/~dogs/clicker/html
www.click-l.com

The ClickerSolutions and ClickSport e-mail lists on yahoogroups are friendly and helpful.

Clean Run®

THE MAGAZINE FOR DOG AGILITY ENTHUSIASTS

Class Ideas for Agility Instructors

Exercises for Backyard Trainers

Course Analyses

America's #1 Source of Dog Agility Information Since 1995!

Training Problems: Cures and Prevention

The #1 agility resource for all levels of trainers and competitors since 1995

> Training and handling techniques from foundation to finish
> Training plans and class ideas for agility instructors
> Exercises to fit every need — from backyard trainer to agility champion
> Ideas for training without equipment
> Course analyses — what worked, what didn't

> Training problems: their cures and prevention
> Discussions of current rules and rule changes
> Major event coverage
> Changes and trends in USDAA, AKC, and NADAC agility
> Developments and news in international agility

One-Year Subscription: $48 in the U.S. • $54 in Canada • $72 Overseas
Subscribe Online: www.cleanrun.com
Call: 800.311.6503 or 413 532.1389 outside the U.S.

Don't let obstacles stand in your way, subscribe today!

- -

Undecided? Mail this card for a free trial issue!

Name

Address

City   State   Zip

Country   Phone or Email

How did you hear about Clean Run?

Place this card in an envelope and mail to: ***Clean Run***
35 N. Chicopee St. Unit 4
Chicopee, MA 01020